The Rise of the Book Plate

Also from Westphalia Press

westphaliapress.org

The Rise of the Book Plate

An Exemplative of the Art

by W. G. Bowdoin and
Henry Blackwell

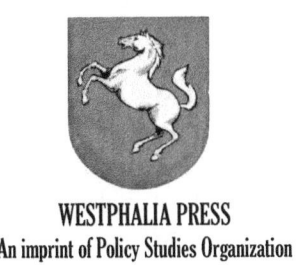

WESTPHALIA PRESS
An imprint of Policy Studies Organization

Westphalia Press
An imprint of Policy Studies Organization
1527 New Hampshire Ave., NW
Washington, D.C. 20036
info@ipsonet.org

ISBN-13: 978-1-63391-622-7
ISBN-10: 1-63391-622-7

Cover design by Jeffrey Barnes:
jbarnesbook.design

Daniel Gutierrez-Sandoval, Executive Director
PSO and Westphalia Press

Updated material and comments on this edition
can be found at the Westphalia Press website:
www.westphaliapress.org

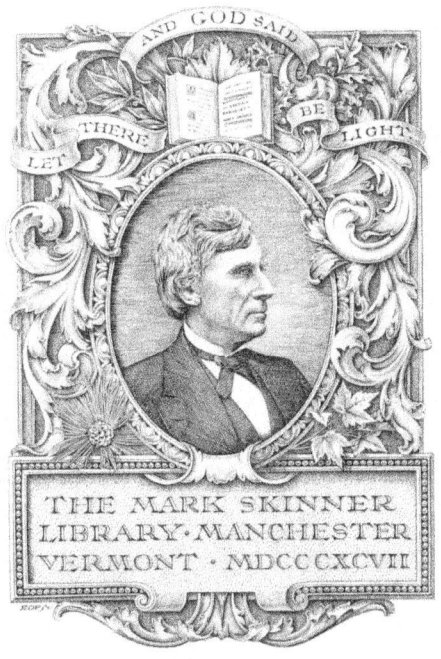

THE RISE OF THE
BOOK - PLATE

BEING AN EXEMPLIFICATION OF THE ART,
SIGNIFIED BY VARIOUS BOOK-PLATES,
FROM ITS EARLIEST TO ITS MOST RECENT
PRACTICE. ILLUSTRATED BY REPRODUCTIONS
IN MINIATURE AND OTHERWISE. TEXT BY

W. G. BOWDOIN

WITH AN INTRODUCTION AND CHAPTER ON
THE STUDY AND ARRANGEMENT OF BOOK-
PLATES BY HENRY BLACKWELL.

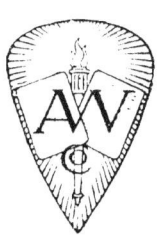

PRINTED FROM THE ORIGINAL COPPER
of Mr. E. D. FRENCH

TO

HAMILTON HOLT,

ONE OF THE EDITORS OF THE "INDEPENDENT,"

FROM WHOM I HAVE HAD

NO LITTLE AID, COUNSEL, ENCOURAGEMENT AND PATRONAGE,

IN MY WANDERINGS IN THE WORLD OF LETTERS,

THIS VOLUME IS DEDICATED

BY THE AUTHOR.

CONTENTS

INTRODUCTION

D
URING the past ten years much has been written about book-plates; a good deal of repetition, seldom anything new, simply the oft-repeated tale dished up in various styles to suit the whims and oddities of the writers. There are more collectors of book-plates to-day than at any other previous time. Many collect because it is the fashion; others again for the money they think there is in it; some because they really admire these artistic bits of paper; and a few in order that they can get together a large collection.

In spite of the strictures of unthinking critics, however, there is much that can be urged in favor of book-plate collecting. It is not so easy to obtain examples of the rarer varieties now as it was in the days about which W. J. Hardy writes so pleasantly, but there are still rewards for the patient collector who is untiring in search. Book-plate collecting, aside from being educational, is a means of social relaxation, and there is something to be said in favor of the exchange of personal plates on the part of collectors who are strangers one to the other.

More knowledge is requisite for the book-plate collector of our day than was needed in the equipment of the pioneers in the field, and the literature available upon the subject is constantly increasing. Countries again that once sat in darkness are coming more and more to book-plate light. Book-plate designers spring up on every hand, and the total number of existing book-plate examples is simply bewildering. Many of them are, of course, common-place, but many a gem is encountered among the modern or so-called "recent" products.

The aim in the volume that now comes from the hand of Mr. Bowdoin is not to pull down book-plate card houses, but rather to add something to the sum of book-plate knowledge, to help those who would be collectors to a little more acquaintance with book-plate lore, and to some extent to lighten their toil in their search after ex-libris wisdom. His list of the more recent American engravers and designers of book-plates will be found to contain many new names, but he has not by any means assembled them all.

From my own personal standpoint I am constantly gaining, rather than losing, interest in the subject. I welcome any serious publication regarding it, and I do not believe that I stand in a state of isolation in regard to it.

HENRY BLACKWELL.

THE STUDY AND ARRANGEMENT
OF BOOK-PLATES.

THE collector who appreciates art, as well as the joy of collecting, finds book-plates unusually fascinating, something in fact totally different from any other hobby, and the more interested he gets the deeper he becomes involved in his pursuit. With each addition to his collection, he should be able to tell at a glance if he already has it, to what nation it belongs, and to form a good idea as to who engraved or designed it, be it ancient or modern.

The age of a plate that is not dated can, by the expert collector, be told with a great deal of certainty; even by the amateur it is not hard to determine, as plates have their own individuality and characteristics at stated periods.

To study book-plates thoroughly means that you must have a knowledge of heraldry, geography, genealogy, and biography, be the possessor of a good library on all of these subjects, and have familiarity with everything that has been published on the subject.

Oftentimes the collector gets a plate that is a puzzle to him. It looks as if it were American, but it may be an English example, or possibly a Continental ; and to get at the exact particulars of that one plate, hours will be wasted and considerable correspondence involved, all without any result. Very few have any idea of what this one plate means to the collector. Going on the supposition that it is an old American plate, an examination of American biographical works is necessary; then Allibone ; after that lists of graduates of the various colleges, as they are the most likely people to own plates ; if these fail, the Index to American Genealogies may help solve the question. Even the lists of subscribers printed at the end of books published in this country some sixty to a hundred or more years ago are worth preserving, as they contain names of people who bought books, and only book buyers in those days owned book-plates, which cannot always be said to-day.

Frequently one comes across a book-plate that looks foreign, has a foreign name, and is even signed by the name of an engraver well known as a foreigner; and yet, after all, this plate may belong to an American and be the plate of a man who had made a name in American history. Each plate has to be carefully investigated, and the study of the same often leads to surprising results, and makes one familiar with the history of people famous years ago and all forgotten now, their memories being brought to light simply because they had a book-plate fifty to four hundred years ago. In olden times in America as well as in other countries nigh all important people who cared for books had book-plates. Examine any important collection of American plates, and it will be a revelation to discover names of people well known in American history who had such plates. What a grand work would it be if a biographical dictionary of all who had personal plates from the earliest times to the year 1900 could be made. It would contain the greater portion of the famous people in the world's history. Some day it will be done, for the reason that book-plates are thoroughly studied now, and will be more so, year by year.

The serious collecting of book-plates means a great deal in these days. Plates are hard to get, particularly old varieties; and there is no limit to the money you may spend. Big collections cannot be gathered as easily as was the case ten years ago, unless by purchasing collections formed by others, and that cannot really be called true collecting. To know what you have and something about them, it is better to gather singly, or a few at a time, then you can learn as you go along. Experience teaches in book-plates quite the same as in other branches of collecting.

Regarding the number of book-plates of all nationalities known to collectors, it is difficult to give an accurate estimate, but I should judge the number may reach some two hundred thousand; and in collecting it is advisable to make up one's mind as to the branch one will collect. In America it is better to collect only Americans, and in England English, and collectors in each country should confine themselves to their own nationality. If one insists on a mixed collection, it only makes one's task more arduous and exasperating in determining to what country they belong.

When one is fairly started the question arises, How shall I keep my plates? This is a knotty question, and not always satisfactorily answered; each collector has his own idea on the subject: some keep their plates in scrap-books, others in cigar boxes and envelopes. For my part I have tried many ways, and discarded all for the reason that they gave too much trouble, and difficulty in finding a plate when wanted, unless one had a card index, and that again entailed too much work. The idea in arranging plates, particularly when they run into the thousands, is to so have them that any certain plate can be found at a moment's notice, and to do this I have adopted the single-mount plan. I use a thick gray-tint linen paper, as that color shows the plate to the best advantage; the mount is 6 x 10 inches, as this size will admit of two ordinary plates. I paste the two upper corners of the plates about an eighth of an inch and then put in position on the mount. If one does not want to paste the corners, the plate can be put into position by the ordinary postage-stamp gummed hinge, easily obtained from any stamp dealer. I keep all my American, Canadian, English, Welsh, and Continental plates entirely distinct from each other, and all are arranged in *strictly alphabetical order, regardless of style,* ancient and modern, dated or signed. These mounts are all kept in book-shaped boxes 6½ x 10½ inches in size, by 2 inches in thickness; the backs are rounded like a book and covered with morocco with cloth sides. Each box is open in the front; top and bottom are solid. I use a different color of morocco for each series of plates — American in green, English slate color, and so on. The backs are neatly finished and lettered "American Book-plates, Vol. 1, 2, 3," and upward, "English Book-plates, Vol. 1, 2, 3," and as high as they go. In order that I may know exactly what the contents of each box is, I take a small piece of paper and mark on "Vol. 1, A–BAC, Vol. 2, BAD–CONN," and so on right through the alphabet. If I want to add a plate or examine one I look at my little slip of a paper index which is pinned on the door or wall, and see what box or volume I will find it in, turn the box and all will come out in my hand; get what I want, put it back in the box and then in its proper place on the shelf. If I add further boxes to any series I rearrange the plates by dividing up, make a new index and destroy the old one. When the boxes are on the shelves they look like so many sets of books, and always appear neat and tidy. I find this arrangement so simple and effective that I can go to my book-plate book-case in the dark, strike a match, look at the index, and get what I want, all in a moment. After a collecting experience of over twenty years, I think the plan I have adopted excels any I have seen, and I would strongly advise all collectors to go and do likewise.

.HENRY BLACKWELL.

THE RISE OF THE BOOK-PLATE.

S O much hostility to the collectors of book-plates has recently been developed in some quarters that the question may well be asked, are book-plates really deserving of the laborious research given to them, the art lavished upon them, the patient and loving study that has been bestowed upon them? Are they the "dead leaves" of M. Henri Bouchot? Should we look upon them only as trifles, unworthy of serious consideration, or have they a story to tell us, worthy the telling? Finally, shall we collect them?

It would seem that these little bits of the graver's art are not entirely unworthy. As the birds and reptiles of the Trias left their footprints upon the shifting sand of the period, which now remains in rock-form, preserving the careless and capricious track-imprints, so book-plates have lingered hidden in odd volumes, and from them, as chance brings them forth, we may gather certain knowledge of art, history, biography, politics, heraldry, and other flowers in the garden of knowledge that were otherwise forgotten. They and those who collect them have a place in the world in spite of the strictures of many misguided critics.

Book-plates have many and various conceptions, according to the artists who wrought them, and a striking contrast is presented between the plate of Hildebrand Brandenburg of 1480 and a current plate from the hand of any one of our best book-plate artists. The period of book-plate history covers at least 400 years, and if we allow the legendary claims of Japan to priority in the use of book-plates, the extent of the period is at once very largely expanded. Collectors generally have not yet reached the point, however, where they may safely go back to the tenth century as the dawn of the book-plate. It is safer, less nebulous, and much more satisfactory to allow to Germany her claim of introducing the indication of book-ownership by means of them. Printing and book-plates may, without violence, be considered cognate, or nearly so. Certain it is that, with the introduction of printing, a field for book-plate use and usefulness quickly arose, and was soon firmly established.

The earliest book-plates were, many of them, certainly very crude, when measured by present-day standards. Crudeness in art form cannot, however, be urged against those derived from Dürer, Jost Amman, Hogarth, and some others who were workers, from whose hands came book-plates. The creation of early book-plates was, however, not all in the hands of such masters. Other and less able artists there were whose products, while full of interest, because of antiquity or for other reasons, are anything but beautiful.

The rise of the book-plate was followed by immediate popular favor in its behalf, and the transition from the simple typographical label to the more artistic forms was speedy. Following the label we have, in rapid sequence, according to the very generally recognized artistic nomenclature devised by Warren, and somewhat amplified by others, varying armorial and heraldic types, the Jacobean, Georgian, Chippendale, or Rococo, Ribbon and Wreath or Festoon, the Celestial, Allegoric, and finally the Pictorial, which includes the Book-pile, Library Interior or corner, Landscape as best exemplified possibly by Bewick, Architectural, Portrait, Urn, Ruin, and picture-forms not all of which are as yet officially classified.

The mission of the book-plate was, is, and will always be to indicate the ownership of the books in which they find a place — lest we forget. If there was only one way in which this could be done, all book-plates would be alike; but diversified possibilities of art interpretation arise, so that an endless variety is easily one of the features of book-plates. A book-plate is again representative of the owner, and symbolizes him in a certain way, as his visiting card and his note-paper do otherwise and otherwhere. These standards of representation were tinctured or colored during the prevalence of the Jacobean, the Chippendale, or other period with those prevailing forms that were for the moment current. One form succeeded another, and, particularly in France, political history is frequently written on a man's book-plate, as testimony is also borne to the belief in the fabulous animals of mythology that are imprinted upon many book-plates that are now interesting chapters in book-plate zoology.

There seems also to be a kind of national flavor about book-plates, so that an English plate would not easily be mistaken for a French or German plate, and an American plate differs from an English, Russian, Spanish, Bavarian, or any other kind. The identification of what is known among collectors as an anonymous plate, that is to say, an armorial or other plate not bearing the owner's name, is not always an easy task. It signifies much research and some considerable familiarity with book-plate styles, as well as artists and the dates when they flourished.

The veteran collector, with an ample reference library and a wide knowledge of history and heraldry, is sometimes unable to solve the problem, and if the professors fail, where shall the inexperienced student appear? If, perchance, the book-plate maker has happily signed the plate, the difficulties are greatly lessened, for the plate must belong to the period bounded by the life of the engraver. A plate of the Chippendale style and period must be identified with an owner who was contemporaneous with the currency of the Chippendale book-plate, which was approximately from 1730 to 1780, and so on. The magic keys, in unlocking such secrets and leading to plate identification, are long-continued patience and industry, combined with enthusiasm that is undying. Thus the closed doors are opened and the unknown plate is identified, otherwise not.

The Germans are great producers of book-plates. They are also fond of the use of color in their plates, which they succeed in introducing by means of lithography, which is constantly employed by them in the production of book-plate forms in which the grotesque element finds great popularity. Joseph Sattler is one of the most notable German figures as a book-plate designer. Many of his plates are exceedingly rich in point of color and color combination. A pronounced humor is, as well, easily characteristic of Sattler's plates.

Book-plates are very popular in France. They did not come into use in that country, however, so early by a hundred years as in Germany. There is an art delicacy that is characteristic of a good French plate that neither Sattler nor any other German artist can approach. Revolutions and political events influence French book-plate designs of the period between the close of the eighteenth and the advent of the nineteenth century that lend to them a special interest not present in the plates of any other country.

The influence of the first Napoleon extended to as small a detail as the frequently unconsidered book-plates of France. It is to him that we owe the origination of the toque, designed by Louis David, and surmounting the escutcheon by means of the color modification of which, in connection with ostrich plumes, various in number, rank was indicated, instead of by means of the modified helmet and its barred vizors open, closed, in profile, etc., etc.

In modern French book-plates, as in their salon pictures, the nude female figure finds a frequent place. Neither Swiss nor Italian plates are especially noteworthy. Many Spanish examples lurk as yet undiscovered in old Castilian volumes. The sharp eye of the collector who searches them out will work in a field almost unexplored, and he will have his just reward. There are some few Russian plates, but Russian art has, for the most part, been employed in producing objects other than book-plates. Whatever she may have had in the way of such achievements is borrowed in *motif* almost entirely from the more versatile French of the Louis XVth period. None of her book-plate products have as yet been artistically notable. In Austria there are a few names in connection with book-plates that have stood out most conspicuously in the past. According to Wilhelm Schölermann, a recent authority, these are Dietl, Yunker, Kenckel Konperz, Nicolai, C. Dietell (of Graz), Alois Count Rosée, Fr. Mayer, and Fr. Schauer (the engraver).

There are but three modern Austrian book-plate designers of note. These are Ernst Krahl, Hugo Ströhl, and Emil Orlik. Something has been done in Belgium in a book-plate way, and while Belgian book-plates are not common and those that have existence there in collected form are but little known, yet, difficult of access as they continue to be, they have a diversity of style and a careful finish that make them exceedingly interesting, as well as valuable as a department. A. Donnay, A. Rassenfosse, and E. Berchmans, the value of whose poster work has received deserved recognition with the rise of the poster, have turned aside to create some of the best examples of the Belgian ex-libris. In Australia, Norman Lindsay is a new but promising book-plate designer.

The rise of the book-plate has done something more than furnish fuel for the collector's fire. It has encouraged art and craftmanship as nothing else could ever have done. Because of it many artists have not only lived but have made names for themselves in a world naturally cold, indifferent, and easily capable of regarding with unconcern the starvation of one who, with such stimulation as the unobtrusive book-plate can and does furnish, it can load with honors and all but overcome with laudation and panegyric.

Heraldry largely owes its latter-day existence to the book-plate, which has revived and given life to a latent interest in coats-of-arms, their meaning and construction, not to mention their absurdities, that was fast passing, and but for them would have entirely passed. Heraldry once had a greater signification than it is easy for us now to realize. It was then an exact science, and a knight's escutcheon, universally used at tournaments, during the crusades, always and everywhere, was an absolute identification of him. Heraldists found it needful to their prevailing scheme to assign arms to Adam, Noah, Abraham, Moses, and others similar.

Those days are gone, but in the chance book-plate we catch glimpses of the days of chivalry, of the armored knight and his good steed, going forth to right the wrongs that cried out for redress then as now. The armorial book-plate speaks to us of those days and sheds a ray of light that makes the darkness less dense than it would be without this feeble, flickering rushlight. The careful study of the book-plate leads to a better appreciation not only of the suits of armor in which the knights were arrayed as they went up and down the earth inspired by chivalry, but of the motives upon which knighthood was rooted and grounded. We of selfish to-day may well take a book-plate leaf out of the book that tells us of an age when knighthood was in flower and when noble deeds were common without money and without price.

The use of book-plates in America was of course an importation. The early settlers here could not forget the traditions of the mother country. Hence the pioneer American book-plates. For some time we had no native facilities for engraving such plates here. England was, without doubt, the source of origin of the book-plates first used in the American colonies. The first notable essay toward engraving book-plates in the colonies was made in Boston, Mass., by Nathaniel Hurd, who was born in 1730 and died in 1777. Very little more is known of him. He engraved for the most part in the Chippendale style and did some excellent work.

Thomas Johnson, James Turner, and Paul Revere were contemporary workers with Hurd. Of the first two we know only too little. Following those just named were others whose work is now well known to, and highly prized by, collectors. Something like a thousand early American book-plates are known to those to whom the gentle art of collecting appeals. Chief among them all in interest, as well as in value, is the plate of George Washington. It has often been reproduced and copies may easily be had, but an original Washington plate would be cheap at less than one hundred dollars, and even at that price they are not frequently to be met with.

Interest in book-plates rose and fell. During the time of Hurd, and afterward, there seems to have been considerable active interest in the subject. Alexander Anderson, who was the first American wood-engraver, produced a few. Abel Bowen, Joseph Callendar, Henry Dawkins, Nathaniel Dearborn,

Amos Doolittle, E. Gallaudet, Peter Rushton Maverick, and William Rollinson are a few of the others who followed as popular engravers of book-plates.

Subsequent interest appears to have waned, and it was not until about 1850 that the modern revival of book-plates and their production and use seems to have taken place. Even then the interest was not pronounced, and it was not until 1886 that the publication of some articles by Lawrence Hutton in the *Book Buyer* caused something like a proper appreciation of them.

One of the earliest collectors in the United States was the late James Eddy Mauran, of Newport, R. I., whose collection contained, at the time of his death, some 3,500 plates. The British Museum has, perhaps, the finest collection of book-plates in the world. It is certainly the largest. It was a bequest of the late Sir Augustus Wollaston Franks, K.C.B. The Bibliothèque Nationale at Paris has a collection mounted in some sixty volumes folio, but they are ill-arranged, and no attempt has apparently been made to group them according to nationality, style, period, or otherwise, except alphabetically, which is liable of course to bring a Russian plate of the present day next to a fifteenth century German plate or to secure other incongruities equally repellant.

One of the largest American collections, according to a recent estimate, is that of H. S. Rowe, of Boston, the number of whose gathered specimens is put down as approximating 20,000. Miss Maria Gerard Messinger has a notable collection.

Public libraries are coming more and more to give consideration to book-plates. Some have even established collections of plates. Book-sellers no longer give away the bits of paper that signify book-plates, found in old volumes that come into their hands, as they formerly did. Book auctioneers note in their catalogues the presence of a book-plate as an additional charm to a vended book.

The days described by Hardy, when he used to go to a shop in a dingy street, leading off Oxford Street, and there select as many book-plates as were new to his collection at the uniform price of a penny apiece, are no longer with us. One searches in all London in vain for such prices now, and the same is equally true in our own country.

The method of arrangement is a vexed one with many collectors, but the tendency now appears toward the individual and uniform mount. Henry Blackwell, of New York, uses this method in his fine collection and cases the mounts in slip-cover boxes with open front, permitting quick removal and easy comparison of specimens. James T. Terry, of New Haven, Conn., also uses the individual mount arranged and ruled for notes relating to the attached plate.

Public exhibitions of book-plates have been given in Boston, New York, Chicago, and to some extent elsewhere. Something of a wider popular interest in the subject has thus easily been created, and has resulted in an increased demand for and use of such plates on the part of many owners of even small private libraries.

Designs for book-plates appear in the French salons, in the Royal Academy exhibitions in London, and frequently in American art exhibitions. The magazine bibliography is already large and is steadily growing. There is a very considerable class to whom they will never appeal, to whom a book is just like any other merchandise, and it makes no difference how the book is bound —in short, who care for none of these things; but, on the other hand, there are a select few to whom they signify much, and to this company of book-lovers and fanciers, book-plates will reveal more and more of charm, with their present rising that now bids fair to continue.

Book-plate collectors are, generally speaking, exceedingly fraternal. Flourishing Ex-Libris societies exist in London, Paris, and Berlin. An attempt to establish a similar American society was made in 1897, with headquarters at Washington, D. C., but it was unfortunately not permanently successful.

A book-plate is a unique thing. Primarily, as previously pointed out, it indicates ownership of the book in which it appears, truly, but that is not all. It must have an art voice. It stands for something and it may as well be an inspiration toward knowledge acquisition. The book-plate enthusiast cannot help being a book-lover. It is incompatible that he should be an enemy of books.

The rise of the book-plate has not been pernicious. It can never be. Nestling in a book unknown and unseen until the book is opened, whether quaint or commonplace, artistic or otherwise, it speaks with a mute eloquence to all those not absolutely dead to its many lurking charms.

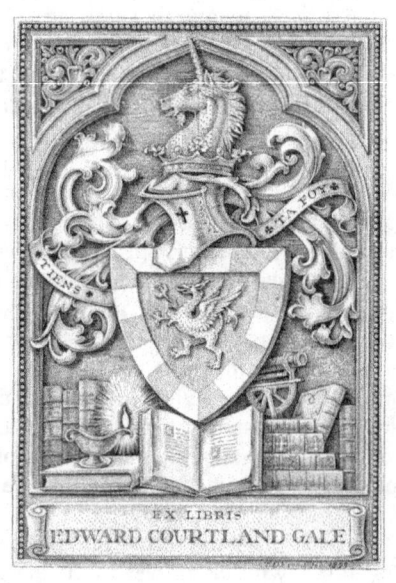

EX LIBRIS
EDWARD COURTLAND GALE

PRINTED FROM THE ORIGINAL COPPER
of Mr. E. D. FRENCH

ON THE SELECTION OF A BOOK-PLATE.

I

THERE was a time when a simple typographical label was all that was required in the way of a book-plate. Stationers, printers, and booksellers kept such in stock with appropriate verses thereon and a blank space that waited for the insertion of a written or printed name therein. This answered the purpose perhaps, but so did the autographic inscription, that is included by the French under the comprehensive term of *ex-libris.*

Many persons speedily arose to whom the typographical label was inadequate. It lacked the distinctive, as well as the artistic quality, the same border frequently recurring ; and to an age, one of whose products was ALBRECHT DÜRER, art doubtless had even a greater significance than with us, with all our achievements and progress, of which we love to boast.

The diffusion of learning was restricted in the beginning of book-plate history, but heraldry was triumphant, and a man was better known by his pictured arms than by his name, which not all could read and spell. Heraldry lent to the earliest book-plates a distinction that we of America, in this day and generation, do not properly appreciate, not alone because of a kind of antipathy to things heraldric, but also because of the decline of our knowledge of this old-time science.

In the early days of printing, which made a place for the book-plate, heraldry bounded the horizon, and after the plain label, a man wishing a book-plate placed his arms thereon and the thing was finished. To-day a broader field lies before the man who contemplates the choice of a book-plate; casting aside the armorial, a thousand art forms yet remain to him to minister to his taste and to offer him that which shall be a mark of individuality.

It is not easy to select that which shall thus fittingly represent the man and stand for him symbolically, without violence and without offence. The recent exhibition held at the Boston Museum of Fine Arts has revived current interest in the subject of book-plates, but one is bewildered at the multitudinous variety encountered at such a place.

The Allegoric has a certain blandishment, but it is often weighed in the balance and found wanting. The portrait plate suggests the pedant, and savors of conceit. The book pile finds those who criticise. The library corner or interior can be made attractive with proper treatment, which is also true of most of the other possible book-plate forms. So likewise with the landscape plate and some · others, but if there be a particularly pleasing present-day tendency, it is undoubtedly toward what is called the pictorial. The selection of some art bit, that tells a story, that speaks without words, that, it would seem, is the ideal plate. Many seek, but few find.

No matter what the medium may be, whether steel, copper, wood, stone, or zinc; whether engraved, etched, lithographed, photo-engraved, or produced by other means, the result often disappoints. The longed-for ideal is missed, and some men have multifarious plates because of this, and disappointments that thus arise. In a matter where such a variety of taste is possible, it is hard to point out that which shall be a guide for all. A Hogarth plate is interesting and artistic: many would rejoice if it were possible for them to have a Hogarth plate, but it migh⸝ not appeal to, and stand adequately for, some others who are equally good ciᴛ ᵣens.

Few men can, oᶠ themselves, absolutely create their own plates. They must have art interpretation of their ideas. The influence of the designer and engraver consequently becomes very great. Much can be gained by the examination of the plates of others. Ideas are thus suggested, and inspirations arise that may be turned to good account. There is, and must ever be, something very pleasing in a book-plate and its quiet unobtrusiveness; it stands with its silent record of ownership, as it were, "like a sentinel who has perished at the post of duty," constantly warning the borrower of his procrastination. A book-plate of itself is not much in the world, but now and then, it yet signifies a great deal. It happens more frequently than we think that it is the things small and weak that overmaster and put to confusion the strong and the mighty ones. A book, no matter how utterly insignificant it may be, in which a George Washington plate undoubtedly appears, suddenly has a value added to it, before which the value of the book without the identifying plate is zero.

Sometimes to the art fabric of the book-plate is added the charm of color, and black and white do not remain alone in combination, but prismatic drafts are made that are set forth in gorgeous array, and to the design mass is added the color mass. The book-plate implies the sometime lending of books (nearly always an unsatisfactory experience, with apologies to GROLIER), and provides for mottoes and epigrams bearing on the sins of those who borrow, and return not again. It will be found a most interesting experience to devise and select features for your book-plate, and to synthetize and combine them so that the resultant product shall rise into one satisfactory whole.

One is easily led into the collecting of book-plates when once he has one of his own, for the chances are he will want to see and know what others have that he has not, and harmless pleasure thus comes to him, that those, strangers to such allurements, cannot have, ANDREW LANG to the contrary notwithstanding. It is not always that so happy a choice can be made as that which enters into and constitutes the chief embellishment of the plate of Oliver Wendell Holmes. On his plate appears a section of the "Chambered Nautilus," about which the genial doctor wrote a well-remembered poem. There is no doubt as to the chosen decoration being entirely representative, and it stands altogether as a most admirable selection. Whitelaw Reid introduces into his book-plate a dainty picture of his country seat, surmounted by a shelf of books as a decorative feature. James Phinney Baxter, of Portland, Maine, shows his own portrait, and a corner of his library, on his plate, with a pleasant two-line motto. Francis Wilson has caught and fixed upon his plate the king's jester of old time, with his cap and bells, reading old folios and ancient manuscripts in the library, while the hour-glass marks the unconsidered flight of time. No one but an out-and-out book-lover could devise such an appropriate plate, nor one that so well signifies the owner and his love of books.

John P. Woodbury, of Boston, on his plate, has had recorded his favorite authors on the backs of tall copies of their works, grouped in orderly confusion, together with the portraiture of three sides of his own library, that makes one envy the happy owner shown seated there amid surrounding books and choice art objects.

Once book-plates were few, now they are many, and new ones arise daily. The examples here considered may be multiplied again and again without exhausting the subject, nor will they always, even so, be found to fit the requirements of the seeker after a book-plate of his own. They will afford hints and serve as guides to help him, but that is all. The final joy lies in the complex inspiration of finding out for one's self something new, and not in copying that which has previously been.

SOME OF THE
MORE IMPORTANT RECENT AMERICAN ENGRAVERS
AND DESIGNERS OF BOOK-PLATES.

Edwin A. Abbey
F. Adams
Max Bachmann
Mrs. William Elliot Baillie
Charles I. Berg
E. H. Bernard
W. H. H. Bicknell
E. B. Bird
John G. Bolton
Claude Fayette Bragdon
Frank Chouteau Brown
H. C. Brown
Arnold William Brunner
John H. Buck
E. J. Burrowes
M. T. Callahan
E. B. Campbell
Richard Cathie
Jay Chambers
George Wharton Edwards
Dr. Henry C. Eno
Edwin Davis French
Edmund H. Garrett
B. G. Goodhue
H. E. Goodhue
Frederick W. Gookin
Fred. W. Goudy
George R. Halm
Theodore Brown Hapgood, Jr.
Frank Hazenplug
Samuel Hollyer
Winslow Homer
W. F. Hopson

F. Arthur Jacobson
C. M. Jenckes
Haydon Jones
William J. Jordan
Charles Rollinson Lamb
L. E. Levy
Will H. Lowe
Henry Mayer
Miss L. Beulah Mitchell
Miss B. C. Pease
F. J. Pfister
Miss Prindiville
Howard Pyle
Frank Rathbun
Christia M. Reade
Louis J. Rhead
Bruce Rogers
Albert Rosenthal
J. A. Schweinfurth
Miss Sarah M. Scribner
Howard Sill
Sidney L. Smith
J. Winfred Spenceley
David McNeely Stauffer
Wilbur Macey Stone
H. Warren Tuttle
Thomas Tryon
Charles A. Walker
George Merwanjee White
Thomson Willing
Andrew Kay Womrath
Michael Wolf

A BIBLIOGRAPHY OF BOOK-PLATE LITERATURE.

Allen, Charles Dexter.

American Book-Plates. A Guide to their Study, with examples — with a Bibliography by Eben Newell Hewins. New York and London, 1894.

Ex-Libris. Essays of a Collector, with twenty-one copper-plate prints. Boston and New York, 1896.

Ames & Rollinson.

Book-Plates. New York City, 1898.

Anonymous Author.

Essai de Bibliographie Canadiênne. With addenda of some 300 Canadian book-plates. Quebec, 1895.

Appletons' Annual Encyclopædia for 1898.

Book-Plates. By W. G. Bowdoin.

Arnold, Edward.

Composite Book-Plates, 1897-8. London, 1898.

Benoit, Arthur.

Les Ex-Libris dans les trois évêches. Toul, Metz, Verdun, 1552-1790. Paris, 1883.

Bouchot, Henri.

Les Ex-Libris et les marques de possession du livre. Paris, 1891.

Carlander, C. M.

Svenska Bibliotek och Ex-Libris. 3 vols. Stockholm, 1889-94.

Castle, Egerton.

English Book-Plates, Ancient and Modern. London, 1893.

Craig, Edward Gordon.

Book-Plates. A Booklet of over a dozen examples (some hand-coloured) of Ex-Libris. Designed and engraved by Edward Gordon Craig, and printed on a brown-toned paper. 350 copies only. A few copies on white hand-made paper. At the Sign of the Rose. Hackbridge, Surrey, 1900.

Book-Plates. A set of 45 Ex-Libris Labels. Designed and engraved (23 hand-coloured) by Edward Gordon Craig, including the Book-Plates of Miss Ellen Terry (four designs), Miss Cissy Loftus, Miss Marion Terry, William Winter, John Drew, and James Pryde. At the Sign of the Rose. Hackbridge, Surrey, 1900.

Dempsey & Carroll.

Book-Plates. New York City, 1897.

De Rieffenberg.

De marques et devises mises à leur livres par un grand nombre d'amateurs. Paris, 1874.

Elkington, J. S. C.

Ex-Libris. A Disquisition concerning Book-Plates, with a few remarks on the cult thereof. By J. S. C. Elkington and examples from the pen of Norman Lindsay. Melbourne, Australia, October, 1900.

Eve, G. W.

Decorative Heraldry. A Practical Handbook of its Artistic Treatment. Chapter on Book-Plates. George Bell & Sons. London, 1897.

Fincham, Henry W.

Artists and Engravers of British and American Book-Plates. A book of reference for book-plate and print collectors. New York (and London), 1897.

Fincham, H. W. and Brown, F.R.G.S., James Roberts.

A Bibliography of Book-Plates. Printed for private distribution. Plymouth. 1892.

Franks, F.R.S., V.P.S.A., Augustus W.

Notes on Book-Plates, No. 1. English dated book-plates, 1574-1800. Printed for private distribution. London, 1887.

Gade, John A.

Book-Plates, Old and New. With illustrations. New York, 1898.

Griggs, W.

Examples of Irish Book-Plates from the Collections of Sir Bernard Burke, C.B., LL.D., Ulster King of Arms. Privately issued by his Son. London, 1894.

Eighty-three Examples of Book-Plates from Various Collections. Plates. Privately printed. London, 1884.

Examples of Armorial Book-Plates. Second series. Plates. London (1891), 1892.

Hamilton, Walter.

French Book-Plates. A handbook for ex-libris collectors. London, 1892.

Dated Book-Plates (ex-libris), with a Treatise on their Origin and Development. In three parts, with about 100 illustrations. London, 1895.

Hardy, W. J.

Book-Plates. London, 1893. Second edition, 1897.

Hildebrandt, Prof. Ad. M.

Heraldic Book-Plates. Twenty-five Ex-Libris. Invented and drawn by Prof. Ad. M. Hildebrandt. London, 1894. 2 vols.

Ingold, C. P.

Les Ex-Libris Oratoriens. Paris, 1892.

Joly, L.

Album d'Ex-Libris Rares et Curieux du XVIIe au XIXe Siècle. Paris, 1895.

Ex-Libris Ana. Noticis Historiques et Critiques Ex-Libris Français. Paris, 1895.

Ex-Libris Imaginaires et Supposés de Personnages Célebrès Anciens et Modernes. Album de Trente-cinq Planches Gravées. Paris, 1895.

Kissel, Clemens.

Symbolical Book-Plates. Twenty-five Ex-Libris. Designed and drawn by Clemens Kissel—Mayence. London, 1894.

Labouchere, Norma.

> Ladies' Book-Plates. An Illustrated Handbook for Collectors and Book-lovers. London, 1895.

Leiningen-Westerburg, Count Zu.

> German Book-Plates. Translated by G. Ravenscroft Dennis. Ex-Libris Series. The Macmillan Company, 1901 (announced).

Lemperly, Paul.

> A List of Book-Plates Engraved on Copper. By Edwin Davis French. With supplement plates, 134 to 144, and Index by Arnold Wood. Cleveland, Ohio, 1899.

Mathews, F. Schuyler.

> The Writing-Table of the Twentieth Century. Being an account of Heraldry, Art, Engraving, and Established Form for the Correspondent. With chapter on Book-Plates. Brentano's, 1900.

Moring, Thomas.

> Book-Plates. London, n. d.

> One Hundred Book-Plates Engraved on Wood. The De la More Press, 52 High Holborn, W. C. London, 1900.

> Fifty Book-Plates Engraved on Copper. The De la More Press, 52 High Holborn, W. C. London, 1900.

Poulet-Malassis, A.

> Les Ex-Libris Français, depuis leur origine jusqu'à nos jours. Nouvelle édition revue très-augmentée et ornée de vingt-quatre planches. Paris, 1875.

Rylands, F. S. A., J. Paul.

> Notes on Book-Plates (ex-libris), with special reference to Lancashire and Cheshire examples and a proposed nomenclature for the shape of shields. Plates. Privately printed. Liverpool, 1889.

Seyler, Gustav A.

> Illustriertes Handbuch der Ex-Libris Kunde. Berlin, 1895.

Slater, J. H.

> Book-Plates and their Value. 1 Plate. English and American plates. London, 1898.

Spofford, Ainsworth Rand.

A Book for All Readers.   Chapter on Book-Plates.   G. P. Putnam's Sons, 1900.

Stitt, J. Carlton.

Ex-Libris Exhibition.   Some notes on the decorative treatment of English Ex-Libris from 1574 to 1830, with a list of the Book-Plate Designers of today.   Liverpool, 1895.

Terry, James.

Ex-Libris Leaflets (3).   The Rose family of Suffield, Conn.; Rev. John Tyler, of Norwich, Conn.; and Abraham Pettibone, of Burlington, Conn.   New Haven, Conn., 1896.

Teske, Charles (Editor).

The Book-Plates Ulrick, Duke of Mecklenburgh.   Wood-cuts by Lucas Cranach and other artists, besides several Ex-Libris of some other members of the Mecklenburgh Dynasty.   J. A. Stargardt.   Berlin, 1894.

Thairlwall, F. J.

An index to (Warren's) "A Guide to the Study of Book-Plates." Plymouth, 1894.

Triptych Designers, The.

A Few Book-Plates and other Dainty Devices by the Triptych.   Illustrated.   Edition limited to 250 copies.   New York, October, 1900.

Vester, J. F.

XL Musical Book-Plates, with a list of more than CCC mottoes to be found on this class of Book-Plates.   Frederik Muller & Co.   Amsterdam.

Vicars, Arthur, F.S.A.

(Ulster King of Arms).   Book-Plates (Ex-Libris).   Series I. Library Interior Book-Plates.   Series II. Literary Book-Plates.   Series III. Book-Pile Ex-Libris.   Plymouth.   Reprinted from Ex-Libris Journal for private circulation.   1893.

Vinycomb, John.

On the Processes for the Production of Ex-Libris (Book-Plates). London, 1894.

Lambert (of Newcastle-upon-Tyne), as an Engraver of Book-Plates. Newcastle-upon-Tyne, 1896.

Warnecke, F.

Die deutschen Bücherzeichen (ex-libris) von ihrem Ursprunge bis zur Gegenwart. Mit einem Titelbilde von E. Doepler. d. J. 21 Abbildungen im Text und 26 Tafeln. Berlin, 1890.

Rare Book-Plates (ex-libris) of the XVth and XVIth Centuries. By Albert Duerer, H. Burgmair, H. S. Beham, Virgil Solis, Jost Amman, etc. Edited by Frederick Warnecke. H. Grevel & Co. London, 1894.

A Score of Book-Plates. Designed and drawn by G. Otto. With a preface by Frederick Warnecke. London, 1894.

Warren, John Leicester.

(Lord de Tabley.) A Guide to the Study of Book-Plates (ex-libris). London, 1892.

John Lane; The Bodley Head. New York and London, 1900.

Washington Centennial Catalogue.

New York, 1889. Item 393 gives list of Book-Plates on exhibition for the first time in America.

Zeitschrift.

Berlin, 1891–1900.

A SELECTED LIST OF
AMERICAN PERIODICAL CONTRIBUTIONS
TO BOOK-PLATE LITERATURE.

Art Amateur, The.

Ex-Libris Notes. Illustrated. Check List of American Book-Plates. Vol. XXX., 92, 121, 148, 173. New York, 1894.

American Book-Plates. By Charles Dexter Allen. Reviewed by Henry Blackwell. March, 1895.

Book Buyer, The.

Some American Book Plates. Illustrated. Vol. III., 7-9, 63-65, 112-114, 159-161. New York, 1886. By Laurence Hutton.

Some English Book-Plates. A Review of Mr. Castle's Book. Illustrated. V., 19-22.

Some French Book-Plates. A Review of Mr. Hamilton's Book. Illustrated. V., 65-67. New York, 1893.

Book-Plate Collections. No. 1. By Henry Blackwell. April, 1895.

The Sewall Collection of Book-Plates. No. 2. By Henry Blackwell. May, 1895.

The Dodge Collection of Book-Plates. No. 3. By Henry Blackwell. June, 1895.

The Hewins Collection of Book-Plates. No. 4. By Henry Blackwell. July, 1895.

The Clark Collection of Book-Plates. No. 5. By Henry Blackwell. August, 1895.

The Libbie Collection of Book-Plates. No. 6. By Henry Blackwell. September, 1895.

The Rowe Collection of Book-Plates. No. 7. By Henry Blackwell. January, 1896.

The Charm of Collecting Book-Plates. By F. E. Marshall. March, 1896.

Book-Lover's Almanac, The.

The Art of the Book-Plate, by Henri Pene DuBois, with seven caricature designs by Henriot. The Carroll Book-Plate, by Charles Dexter Allen. Illustrated. New York, 1893.

Booklover, The.

Bookman, The.

The Book-Plate of S.S. Oceanic. October, 1899.

Book Reviews.

American Book-Plates. By Charles Dexter Allen. Vol. II., No. 1, May, 1894. Macmillan & Co.

Bookseller and Newsman, The.

The Collecting of Book-Plates. By W. G. Bowdoin. Vol. XIV., 10. New York, December, 1897.

Joseph Sattler, Book-Plate Designer. Illustrated. By W. G. Bowdoin. Vol. XVI., page 5. New York, March, 1899.

Boston Daily Globe, The.

Early Book-Plates. April 22, 1885. By Richard C. Lichtenstein.

Brooklyn Eagle, The.

Book-Plates. Old and New. A Review of Mr. Gade's Book, by W. G. Bowdoin. Illustrated. Vol. 58, December 3, 1898. Brooklyn, N.Y.

Book-Plates of Brooklyn Book-Lovers. Mrs. Jenny Young Chandler. December 17, 1899.

Chicago Evening Journal.

Blackwell Exhibit of Book-Plates. April 10, 1895.

Christian Union, The.

> The Book-Plate and How to Make It. New York, April 30, 1892. By E. Ireneus Stevenson.

City Mission Record.

> Book-Plates and their Early Engravers. Hartford, Conn., 1888. By Charles Towneley Martin.

Cleveland Plain Dealer, The.

> The Blackwell Book-Plate Exhibit. February 19, 1899.

Cleveland Town Topics, The.

> The Blackwell Book-Plate Exhibit in Cleveland. Cleveland, Ohio, February 18, 1899.

Collector, The.

> Some Historic Book-Plates. Rev. Dr. J. H. Dubbs. V., 151-152, 164-165, 176-177.
>
> German Book-Plates of Pennsylvania. Rev. Dr. J. H. Dubbs. VI., 3-5.
>
> The Book-Plate of Jacob Sargeant. Illustrated. Charles Dexter Allen. Collection of Book-Plates. VI., 29. New York, 1892.
>
> The Lynch Plate. Walter R. Benjamin. IX., 7. Ex-Libris in Germany (S) IX., 8. Commercial Book-Plates. Lancaster Book-Plates. Rev. Dr. J. H. Dubbs. IX., 21-24.
>
> The Study of American Book-Plates, IX., 37. Humorous Book-Plates. The Nack-Plate. Old American Book-Plates. Rev. Dr. J. H. Dubbs. IX., 53-56.
>
> The Matter of Arrangement. The Enoch Pratt Free Library Collection of Ex-Libris. Some Interesting Labels. Rev. Dr. J. H. Dubbs. IX., 69-72.
>
> Shall Americans Assume Badges? Lancaster Book-Plates. Cleansing Book-Plates. Rev. Dr. J. H. Dubbs. IX., 85-88.
>
> Hobbies. The Matter of Exchanges. Book-Hunting. Rev. Dr. J. H. Dubbs. IX., 101-104.
>
> Book-Plates of the Signers of the Declaration. Jenison-Walworth Book-Plate. School-Boy's Couplets. Marks Plates. Rev. Dr. J. H. Dubbs. IX., 117-120.
>
> Shall We Collect Book-Plates? W. G. Bowdoin. IX., 131-132.

Book-Plate of Sophia Penn. Ex-Libris Typothetæ Diaboli. Rev. Dr. J. H. Dubbs. IX., 132-134. Ecclesiastical Book-Plates. Book-worm on Book-Plates. Rev. Dr. J. H. Dubbs. IX., 143-146.

Ex-Libris Societies. English Engravers of Book-Plates. Rev. Dr. J. H. Dubbs. IX., 156-158. New York, 1896.

Book-Plates and Printers' Marks. Ex-Libris Aftermath. Rev. Dr. J. H. Dubbs. X., 4, 5.

Book-Plate Zoölogy. W. G. Bowdoin. X., 39, 40.

Some English Inscriptions on Book-Plates. W. G. Bowdoin. X., 26, 27.

Ladies' Book-Plates. W. G. Bowdoin. X., 52, 53.

Book-Plate Hunting in Europe. Aldine (Mr. George F. Allison).

The Identification of Book-Plates. W. G. Bowdoin. X., 61-64.

Book-Plate Hunting. W. G. Bowdoin. X., 73, 74.

The Pictorial Plate. W. G. Bowdoin. X., 112.

Some Continental Notes on Book-Plates. W. G. Bowdoin. X., 118-120.

French Book-Plates. W. G. Bowdoin. XI., 2-4.

A Plea for Book-Plates. W. G. Bowdoin. XI., 25-26.

A Brooklyn Book-Plate. W. G. Bowdoin, XI., 60.

Hostility to Book-Plate Collecting. W. G. Bowdoin. XI., 89-90.

Book-Plate Collecting as a Hobby. W. G. Bowdoin. XII., 24, 25.

The Book-Plate Art of Joseph Sattler. W. G. Bowdoin. XII., 36.

Inscription on Book-Plate. George Wightwick. XII., 50.

The Modern Tendency in Book-Plate Designing. W. G. Bowdoin. XII., 81. New York, 1899.

Critic, The.

Book-Plates of New England Authors. A Review of Mr. Castle's Book. Illustrated. XIX., 82, 83.

Some American Book-Plates. Illustrated. XX., 88, 89. New York, 1893.

Blackwell Exhibit. March 23, 1895.

Curio, The.

11-17-61-66, 110-114. American Book-Plates and their Engravers. Illustrated. By Richard C. Lichtenstein. New York, 1887.

Club of Odd Volumes, The.

Tenth Anniversary Exhibition (Book-Plates, etc.).   Boston, 1897.

Dial, The.

Private Book-Marks.   A Note of Mr. Hardy's Book.   Chicago, Ill., February 1, 1894.

Elite, The (Chicago, Ill.).

Blackwell Exhibit.   April 13, 1895.

Ex-Libris.

July, 1896, to April, 1897.   Washington, D. C.

Hartford Post, The.

Hundreds of Book-Plates in the Collection of a Hartford Gentleman. Illustrated.   Hartford, Conn., August 19, 1893.

Home Magazine, The.

Something about Book-Plates.   W. G. Bowdoin.   Vol. XII., 169-172. New York.   February, 1899.

House Beautiful, The.

A Few Chicago Book-Plates.   By Richard Shaw.   Vol. I., 138.   Chicago, Ill.   April 15, 1897.

Illustrated American, The.

Blackwell Exhibit.   April 20, 1895.

Independent, The.

Book-Plates: the Bookman's Hobby.   Charles Dexter Allen.   Vol. XLIX., 2.   New York.   December 9, 1897.

Inland Printer, The.

The Book-Plate: Its Literature, etc.   By W. Irving Way.   Illustrated. Vol. XII., 460, 461.   Chicago, Ill.   March, 1894.
The Chicago & Alton Book-Plate.   Chicago, Ill.   January, 1900.

In Lantern-Land.

On Book-Plate Designs.   Vol. I., 74, 75.   Hartford, Conn.   May 6, 1899.

Jamaica Plain News.

Book-Plates. A Review of Mr. Castle's Book. Illustrated. Jamaica Plain, Mass. July 8, 1893.

Journal, The Morning.

Blackwell Exhibit of Book-Plates at Brentano's. New York. March 17, 1895.

Literary Collector, The.

The Book-Plate Vandal. A. J. Bowden. New York. October 1, 1900.

Literature.

Book-Plates. An Account of the Boston Exhibition at the Museum of Fine Arts. By W. G. Bowdoin. New York, November 23, 1898.

Literary World.

The Study of Book-Plates. A Review of Warren. By Rev. Dr. Joseph Henry Dubbs. Boston, Mass. August 13, 1881.

Loan Exhibition of Book-Plates and Super Libros, Catalogue of.

Held by The Club of Odd Volumes at the Museum of Fine Arts. April 25 to June 5, 1898. Boston, Mass.

Magazine of Art.

"Ex-Libris." A Review of Mr. Castle's Book. New York, December, 1893.

New York Times, Saturday Review of Books and Art.

Review of "A Guide to the Study of Book-Plates" (Warren). By W. G. Bowdoin. August 4, 1900.

Nation, The.

Review of Fincham's Book. New York, February 10, 1898.

New England Historical and Genealogical Register.

Early Southern Heraldic Book-Plates. By Richard C. Lichtenstein. XLI., 296. Boston, 1887.

XL., 295–299. Boston, 1886.

Optimist, The.

Anent Book-Plates : Being a Thumbnail History by Jay Chambers. Vol. I., No. 5. Boone, Iowa. January, 1901.

Providence Sunday Journal.

Collecting Book-Plates. By Mrs. E. H. L. Barker. Providence, R. I. November 15, 1891.

Reformed Church Messenger.

Peter Miller's Book-Plate. By Rev. Dr. Joseph Henry Dubbs. Philadelphia, Pa. June, 1889.

Rochester Herald, The.

Blackwell Exhibit. April 21, 1895.

Scientific American Supplement.

Book-Plates of Celebrated Women. A Review of Labouchere's Book. Vol. XLI., 16,797. February 22, 1896.

Studio, The.

Some Recent Book-Plates. Mostly Pictorial. Gleeson White. April, 1897.

British Book-Plates. Gleeson White.

French Book-Plates. Octave Uzanne.

American Book-Plates. Jean Carré.

German Book-Plates. H. W. Singer.

Austrian Book-Plates. W. Scholermann.

Belgian Book-Plates. Fernand Khnopff. London and New York. December, 1898.

Sunday Herald, The.

Many Interesting Types of Book-Plates. Boston. Mass. April 23, 1899.

Sunday Sun, The.

South Carolina Book-Plates. Charleston, S. C. January 4, 1891.

Sunday Times-Herald, The.

Blackwell Exhibit of Book-Plates at Brentano's, Chicago. Chicago, Ill. April 7, 1895.

Tribune, The.

> Blackwell's Exhibit of Book-Plates at Brentano's, New York. March 15 and 17, 1895.

Washington Post, The.

> Blackwell Collection of Book-Plates at Brentano's, Washington, D. C. Washington, D. C. May 19, 1895.

Y Drych.

> Blackwell Exhibit of Book-Plates at Brentano's, New York. Utica, New York. March 21, 1895.

A SELECTED LIST OF
ENGLISH PERIODICAL CONTRIBUTIONS
TO BOOK-PLATE LITERATURE.

Academy, The.

Art Books.   Review of Warren's Book.   London, November 13, 1880.

Antiquary, The.

Vol. I.   Notes on Book-Plates.   75-77.

Book-Plates (W. Hamilton).   117, 118.

Book-Plates.   189.

Notes on Curious Book-Plates.   236, 237.

Another Chapter on Book-Plates.   Alfred Wallis.   256-259.   London, 1880.

Vol. II.   A Supplementary Chapter on Book-Plates.   6-10.

An Essay on Book-Plates (E. P. Shirley).   115-118.

Book-Plates.   133, 272.   London, 1880.

Vols. III. and IV.   77, 106-111.   London, 1881.

Art Journal, The.

New Series, XV., 267-270.   Notes on Book-Plates.   Illustrated.   M. A. Tooke.   London, September, 1876.

Book-Plate Annual, The, and Armorial Year-Book.

A. & C. Black.   London, 1894.

Book-Plate Collectors' Miscellany, The.

A Monthly Supplement to the "Western Antiquary."   Illustrated. Edited by W. H. K. Wright, F. R. Hist. Society.   Plymouth, 1890, 1891.

Bookseller, The.

"A Guide to the Study of Book-Plates." Review of Warren's Book, "A Guide to the Study of Book-Plates." London, October 6, 1880.

Book-Worm, The.

Book-Plates and their Mottoes. 205. London, June, 1880.

A Hunt for Book-Plates in Paris (W. Hamilton). 171-173.

The Avery Book-Plate. 202. London, 1892.

Catalogues of the Annual Exhibitions of the Ex-Libris Society.

London.

Chambers' Encyclopædia.

Book-Plates. New Edition. Vol. II., 309. London, 1889.

Daily News.

Book-Plates, Etc. (Leader on). London, April 29, 1881.

Genealogist, The.

Vol. V. Review of Warren's Book. London, 1881.

Gentleman's Magazine, The.

Remarks on the Invention of Book-Plates. Part II., 613. London, 1822.

Book-Plates (C. S. B.). Part I., 198, 199. London, 1823.

Book-Plates, Ancient and Modern, with Examples. Illustrated. John Leighton, F.S.A. Fourth Series, Vol. I., 798-804. London, June, 1866.

Globe, The.

Book-Plates. W. J. Hardy. London, November 3, 1891.

Book-Plates. London, July 25, 1891.

The Latest Hobby. London, March 29, 1893.

Graphic, The.

The Reader. Review of Warren's Book. London, October 16, 1880.

Library, The.

Andrew Lang. London, 1881.

Notes and Queries.

First Series.

Book-Plates, Whimsical One, VI., 32.
Motto, I., 212.
Early, III., 495. IV., 46, 93, 354. VII., 26. XI., 265, 351, 471.
XII., 35, 114. London, 1849-1855.

Second Series.

Book-Stamps, Armorial, X., 409. London, 1856-1861.

Third Series.

Book-Plates, Armorial. VI., 306.
Their Heraldic Authority. XII., 117, 218. By R. A., wood engraver.
VIII., 308. London, 1862-1867.

Fourth Series.

Book-Plates, Armorial. IV., 409, 518. V., 65, 210, 286. IX., 160.
Exchanged. X., 519. London, 1868-1873.

Fifth Series.

Book-Plate, R. T. Pritchett's, IX., 29, 75.
Query, X., 428.
Book-Plates, Armorial, I., 386.
Exchanged, I., 60, 199. II., 159.
Punning, IV., 464. V., 35.
Handbook of, VI., 465. VII., 36, 76.
Heraldic, VI., 369, 543. VII., 28, 36, 76, 233, 435, 515.
Earliest Known, VII., 76, 235.
Mottoes on, VII., 427. VIII., 111, 258.
Collections, VII., 435, 515. VIII., 38, 79, 118, 158, 178, 360. XI., 260.
Book-Plates. Dated, VIII., 200, 298, 397, 517. IX., 198. XI., 446.
XII., 33.
How to Arrange Collections, IX., 20.
Papers on, IX., 360. London, 1874-1879.

Sixth Series.

Many References. London, 1880-1885.
The Book-Plate's Petition. A Poem. Austin Dobson. January 8,
1881.

Oxford University Archæological and Heraldic Society.

Third Annual Report.   On Book-Plates.   Rev. Daniel Parsons.   Oxford, J. Vincent, 1837.

Palatine Note Book.

Vol. I.   Book-Plates.   15, 16, 30, 52, 53, 69, 114, 195.   Illustrated.   217. Of Jesus Collection.   Camb.   128.
Walpole's.   209.   Manchester, 1882.

Paper and Printing Trades Journal.

Ex-Libris.   Illustrated.   March, page 48.   September, page 19.   London, 1881.

Printing Times and Lithographer.

Curiosities of Book-Plates.   VII., 265-268, 290, 292.   London, 1882.

Publishers' Circular, The.

Book-Plates.   London, August 8, 1891.

Saturday Review, The.

Book-Plates.   Review of Warren's Book.   London, October 20, 1880.
Book-Plates.   A Review of the Ex-Libris Journal.   London, July 25, 1891.

Scottish Review, The.

Book-Plates.   XXI., 315-329.   London, April, 1893.

Tit-Bits.

Who Has the Finest Collection of Book-Plates in this Country?   London, October 21, 1893.

West Middlesex Advertiser, The.

Leaves from a Library on Book-Plates.   Walter Hamilton, F.R.G.S. March 26.   April 2, 9, 16, 23, 30.   May 7, 14.   London, 1881.

BOOK·PLATE INSCRIPTIONS.

I

If thou art borrowed by a friend,
   Right welcome shall he be
To read, to study, NOT TO LEND,
   But to return to me.

Not that imparted knowledge doth
   Diminish learning's store,
But books, I find, if often lent,
   Return to me no more.

Read slowly, pause frequently, think
seriously, keep cleanly, return duly with the
corners of the leaves not turned
down.

> —SAMUEL RANKIN, Baltimore, Md.
> (and many others).

❧

If any one should borrow me,
   Pray keep me clean
For I am not like linen cloth,
   That can be washed again.

❧

As the Sun colors flowers
   So Art colors Life.
> —W. W. CHEVALIER.

Eagles and Books Fly or Sink Alone.

He who lendeth a book taketh chances.
To take chances is to gamble.
It is wicked to gamble.
Kind friend, ye who seek to borrow, tempt me not to sin.
　　　—ARTHUR T. VANCE, New York.

"Go to them that sell, and buy for yourselves."
　　　—D. W. JAYNE.

"The ungodly borroweth and payeth not again."

With welcome use—but use with care;
The wicked borrow—but never return.
　　　—WILLIAM BELCHER, New London, Conn.

The wicked borrow, but do not return again;
See thou art not of that number.
　　　—AARON PUTNAM.

Who loves not knowledge.
Who shall rail against her beauty.
May she mix with men and prosper.
　　　—SAMUEL DAVIS.

Rivers always lead to ports and end as books
do, blending with the sea.

❧

" The pen is mightier than the sword."
—George W. Childs, Philadelphia, Pa.

❧

Who learns and learns, but does not what he knows,
Is one who plows and plows, but never sows.
—James Phinney Baxter, Portland, Maine.

❧

Cherish virtue.
—Sally King.

❧

"Send him back carefully, for you can if you like,
that all unharmed he may return to his own place."
(Suggested by Andrew Lang.

❧

This book was bought and paid for by
D. C. Colesworthy.
Borrowing neighbors are recommended to
supply themselves in the same manner.
Price, seventy-five cents.

❧

A good Book is the Best of Friends, the Same
Today and Forever (Martin Tupper).
—Gilbert North.

My friend! should you this book peruse,
Please to protect it from abuse;
Nor soil, nor stain, nor mark its page,
Nor give it premature old age:
And, when it has effected all,
Please to return it ere I call.

⁂

All the while this eternal court is open to you.
—Paul Lemperly, Cleveland, Ohio.

⁂

"Hold to Nature."
—Charles M. Skinner, Brooklyn, N. Y.

⁂

Reading maketh a full man.
—Edwin S. Crandon.

⁂

Missing.
A book from the library of
J. Bryant.

⁂

"Far more seemly were it for thee to have
thy Study full of bookes than thy
purses full of mony" (Lilly).
—Samuel Putnam Avery, N. Y.

48

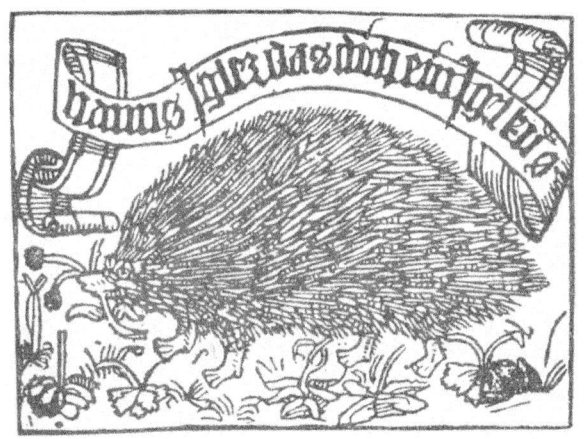

Book-Plate of HANS IGLER.   Circa 1450
Has been considered as the earliest known book-plate

[GERMAN]

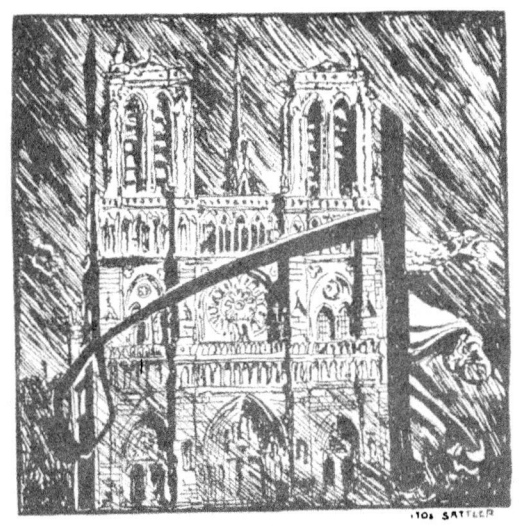

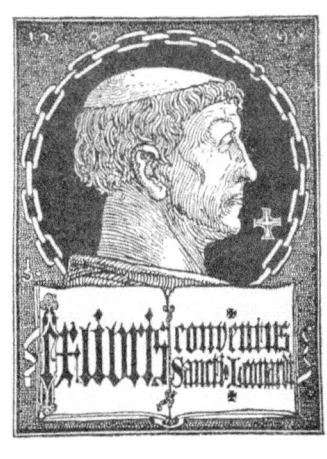

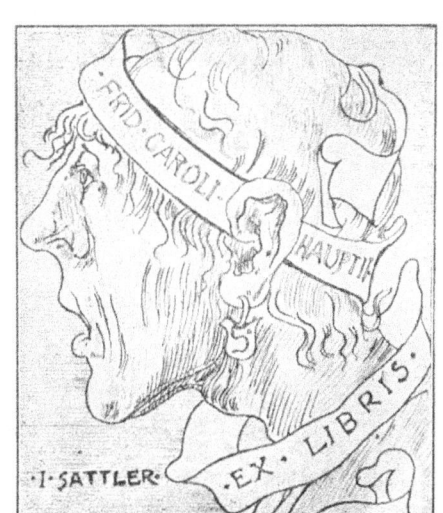

Designed by Joseph Sattler

51

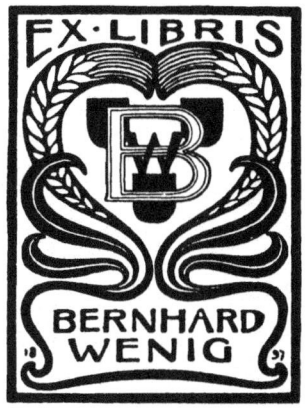

BY BERNHARD WENIG
German

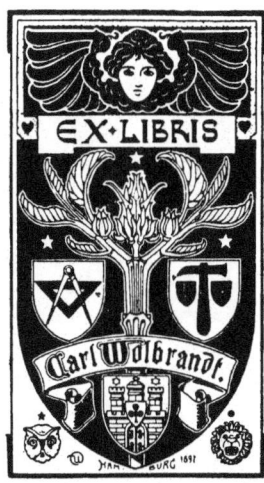

BY CARL WOLBRAND

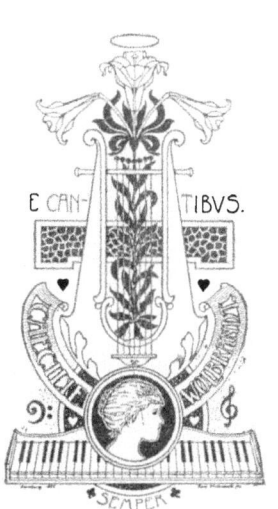

BY CARL WOLBRAND

[GERMAN]

53

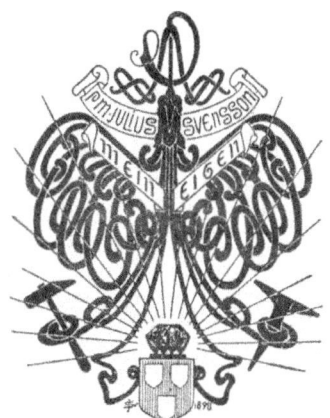

BY JULIUS SVENSSON

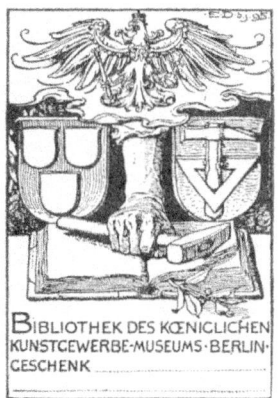

BY DOEPLER
German

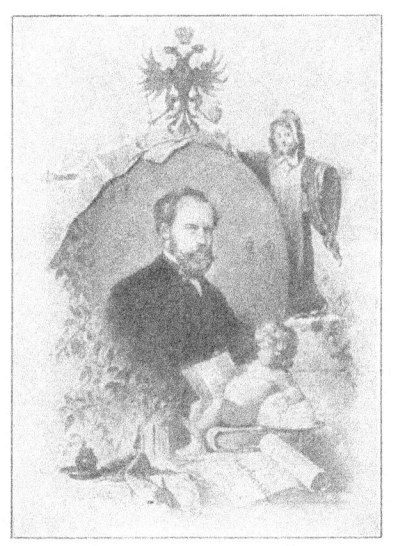

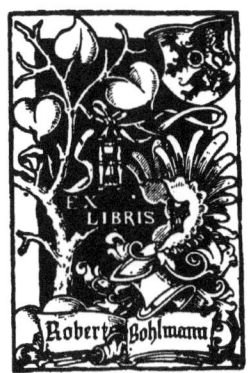

BY HILDEBRANDT

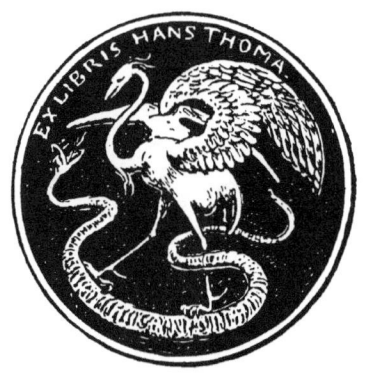

BY HANS THOMA

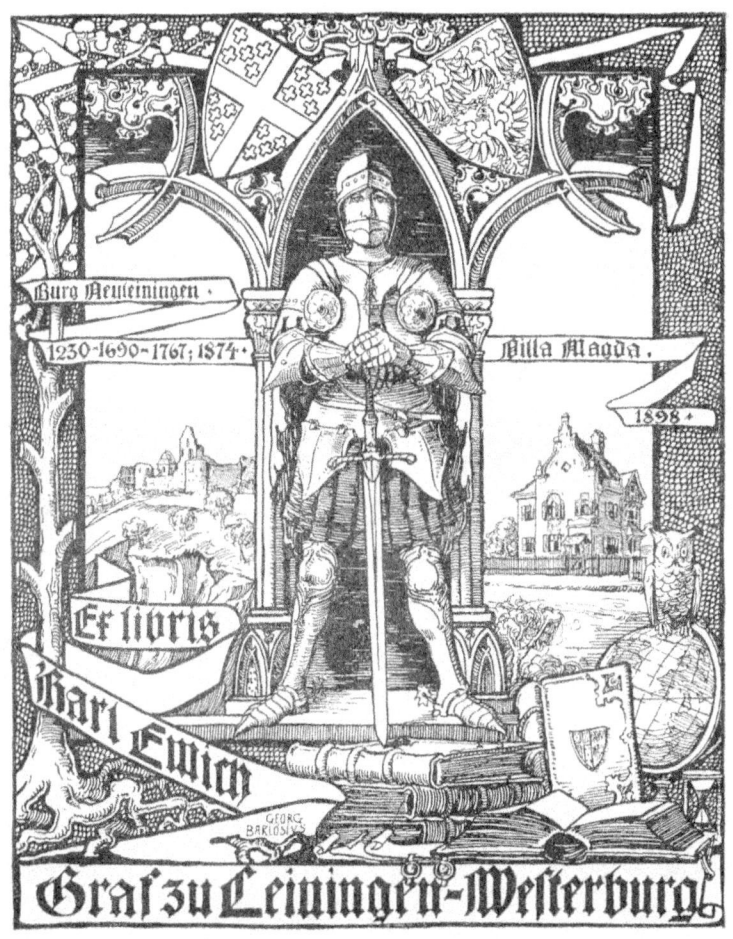

Designed by GEORG BARLOSIUS

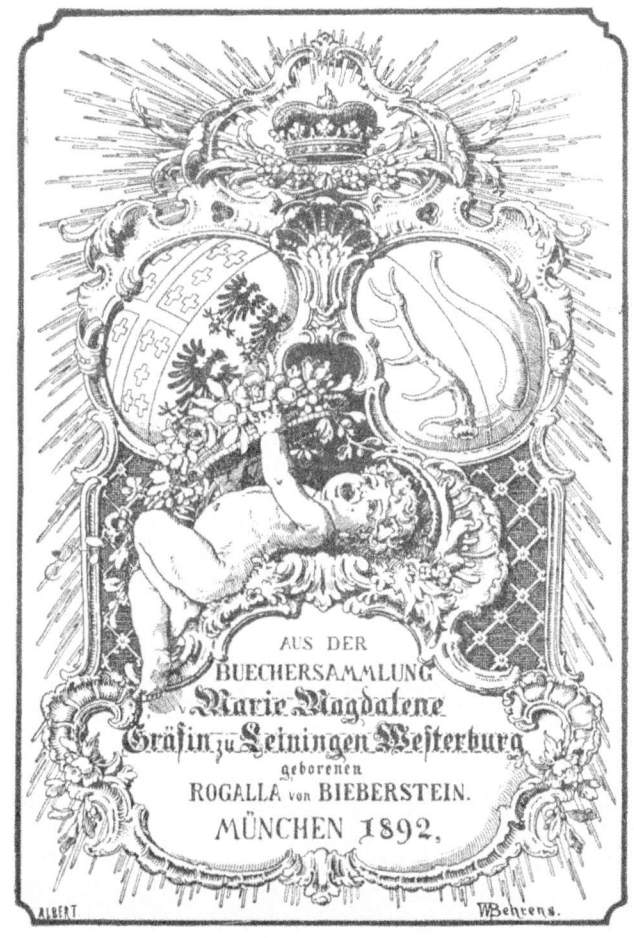

Designed by W. Behrens

[GERMAN]

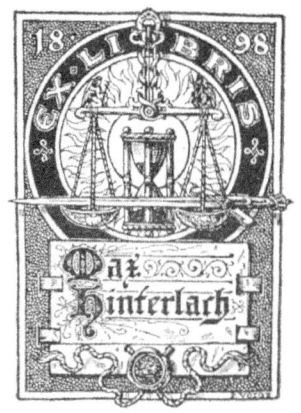

BY PAUL VOIGT

Austrian

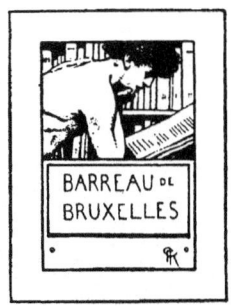

BY FERSAND KHNOPFF

Belgian

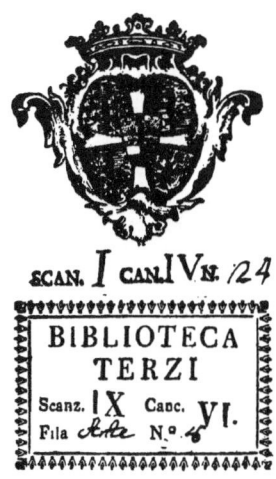

SCAN. *I* CAN.*I* V.*N. 124*

BIBLIOTECA
TERZI
Scanz. IX   Canc. VI.
Fila *Alta*   N.º *4*

Neapolitan Book-Plate — Native Design

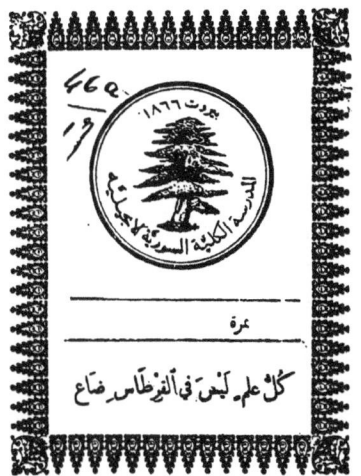

Native Design

69

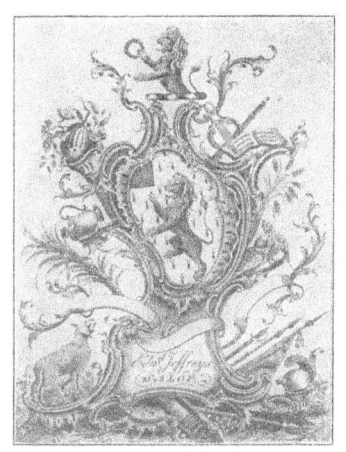

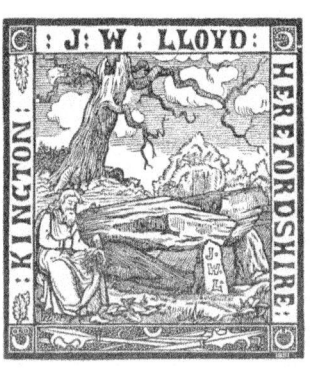

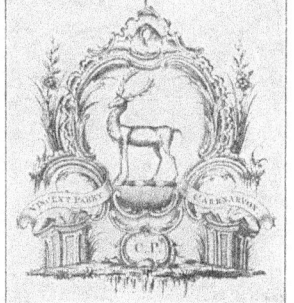

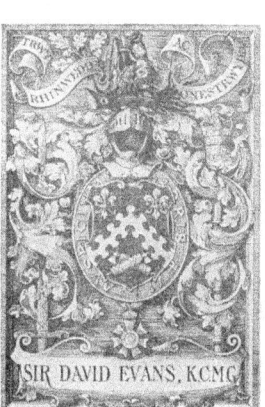

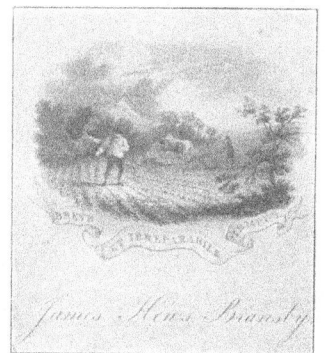

Various Designers

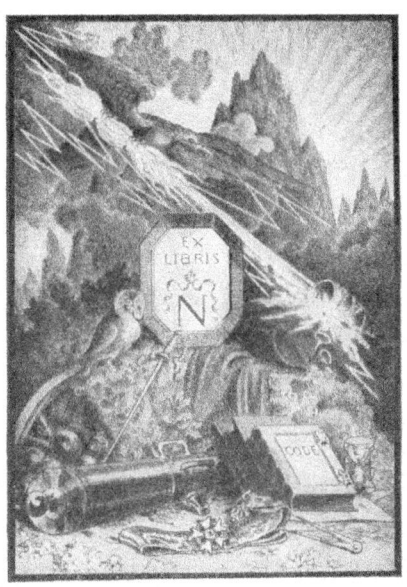

Ex-Libris Imaginaires Napoléon I

Designed by M. L. Joly

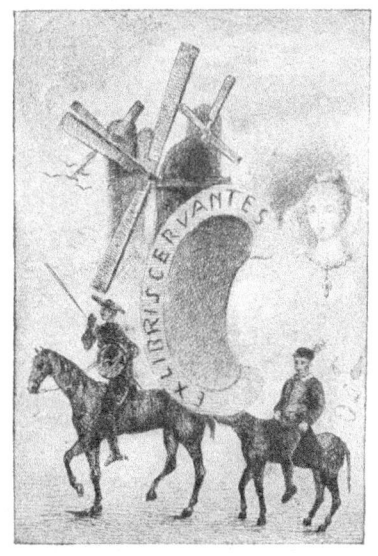

Ex-Libris Imaginaires Cervantes

Designed by M. L. Joly

73

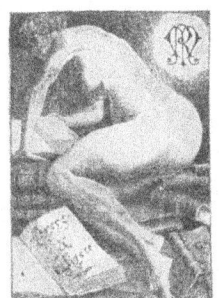 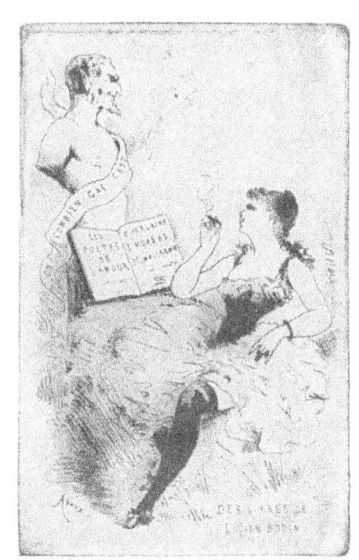

Designed by Apoux

75

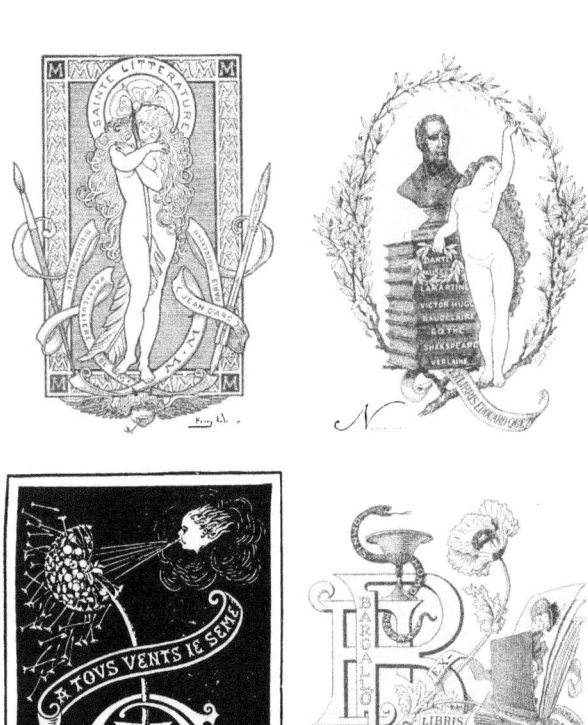

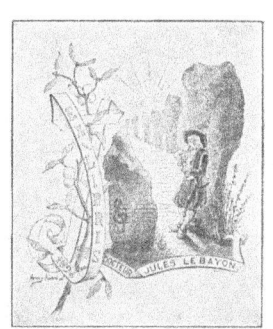

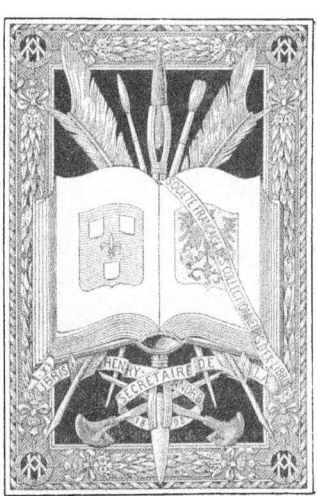

Designed by Henry André, Paris

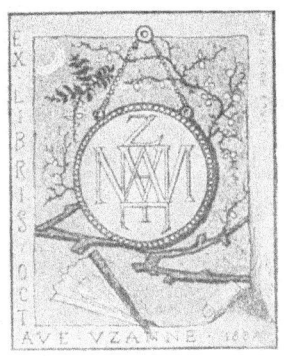

Designed by AGLAÜS BOUVENNE

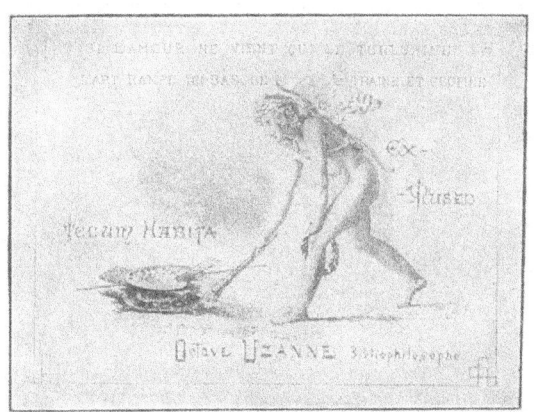

OCTAVE UZANNE

French Author Plates

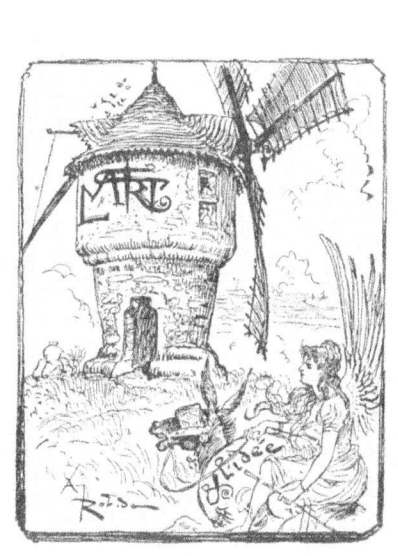

BY A. ROBIDA

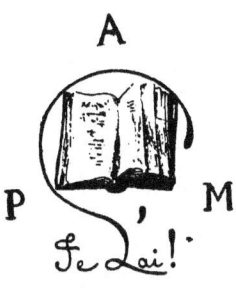

BY BRACQUEMOND

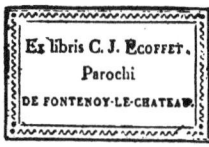

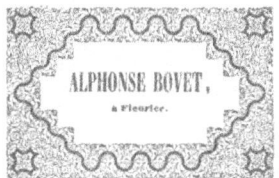

French Label Book-Plates

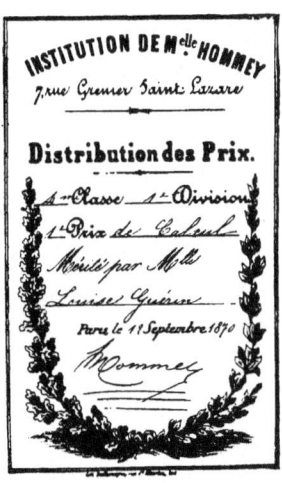

French Prize Labels

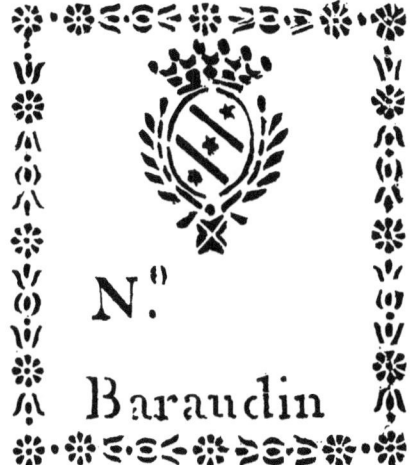

Stencilled Book-Plate

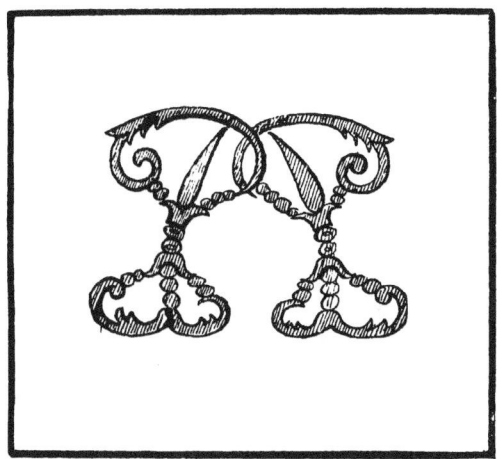

Book-Plate of Philippe I, Duc d'Orleans

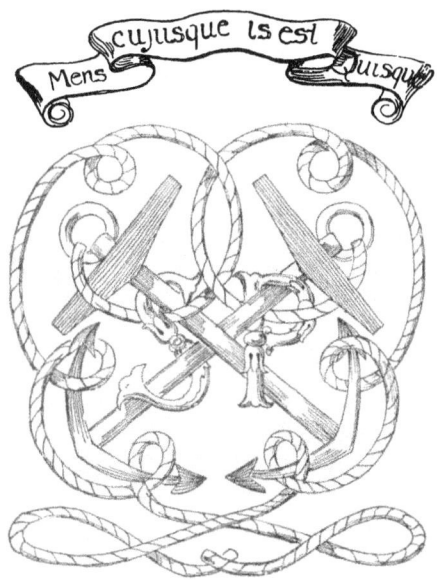

Book-Plate of Samuel Pepys.

(He had two others)

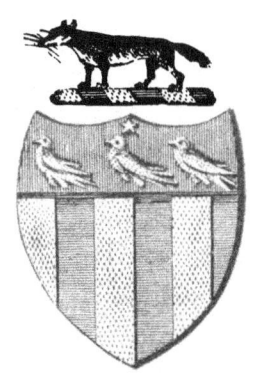

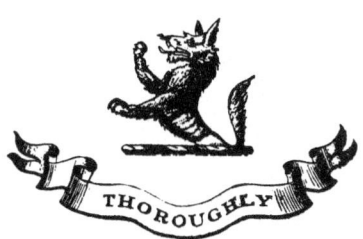

Sidney Woolf,
Middle Temple.

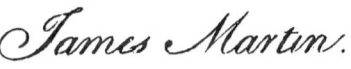

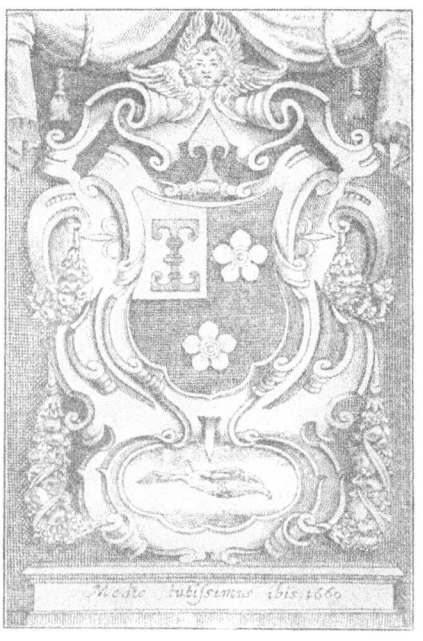

Only one other copy of this plate known.
It is in the British Museum.

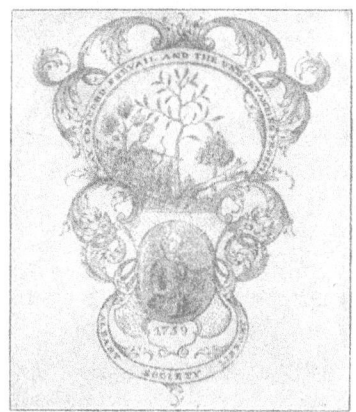

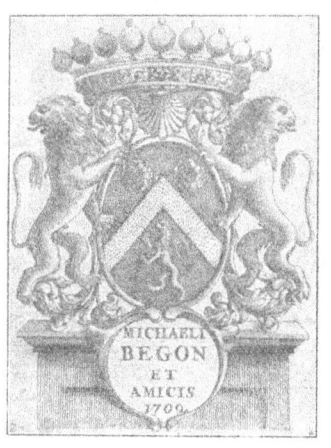

Early Dated Plates

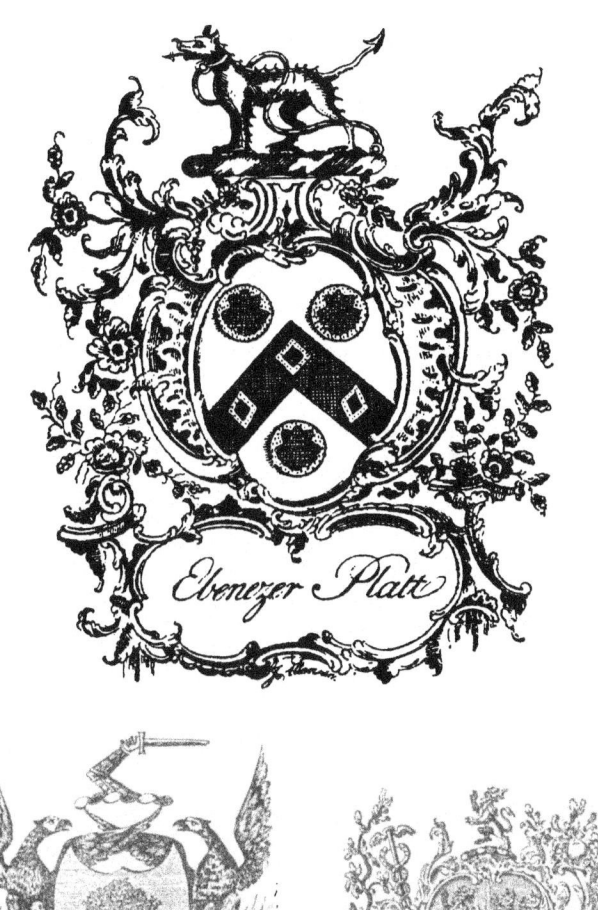

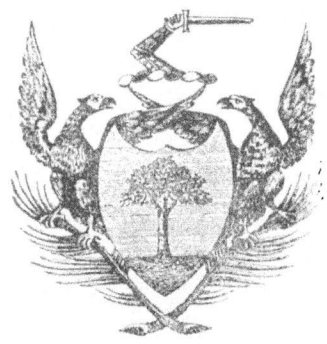

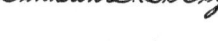

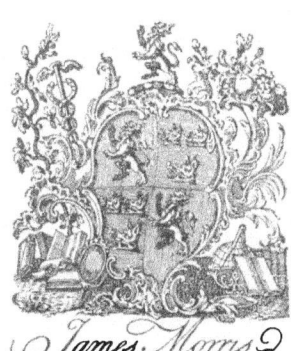

American

Designed by George Bickham, London

Early Armorial Book-Plates

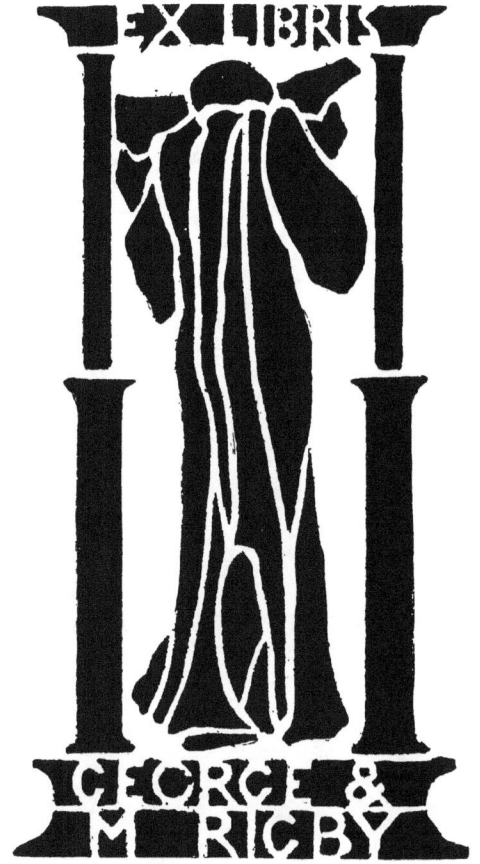

A Stencilled Book-Plate

Designed by GEORGE R. RIGBY

[ENGLISH]

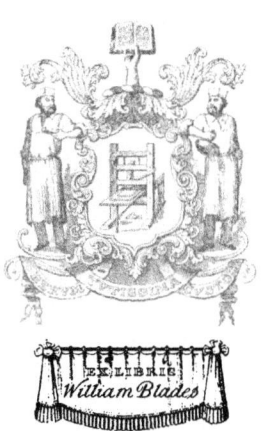

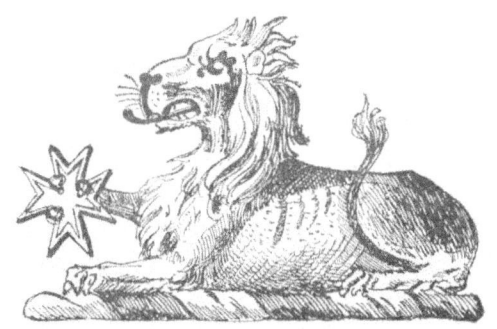

Book-Plate of Charles Dickens

(Somewhat Enlarged)

Original is a beautiful Steel-plate

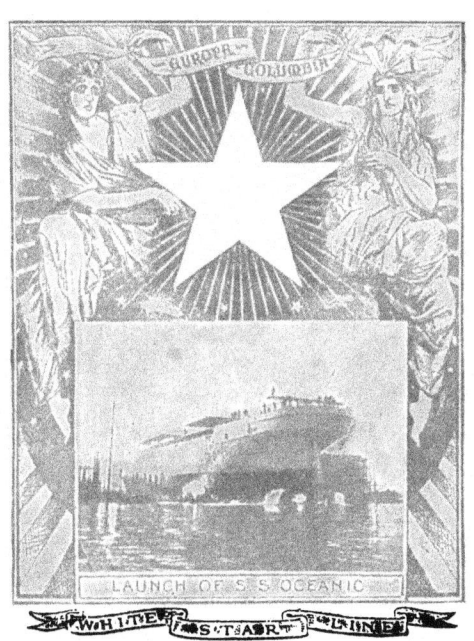

LAUNCH OF S. S. OCEANIC

WHITE STAR LINE

Book-Plate used in the Library of the S. S. Oceanic

Designed by LINLEY SAMBOURNE, one of the Artists of Punch

Original is a Photogravure

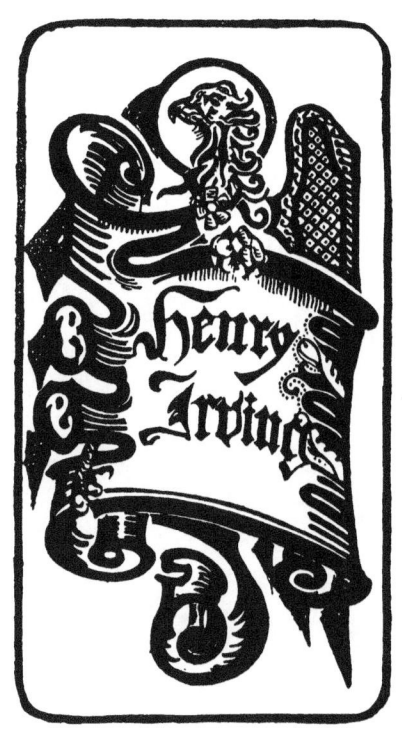

Book-Plate of Sir Henry Irving

Original in Black and Red

Designed by BERNARD PARTRIDGE

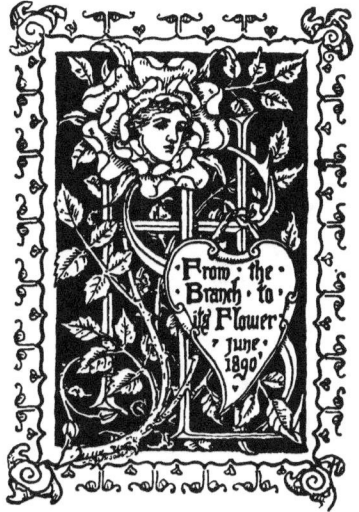

BOOKPLATE OF MISS MAY MORRIS : DESIGNED BY Walter Crane.

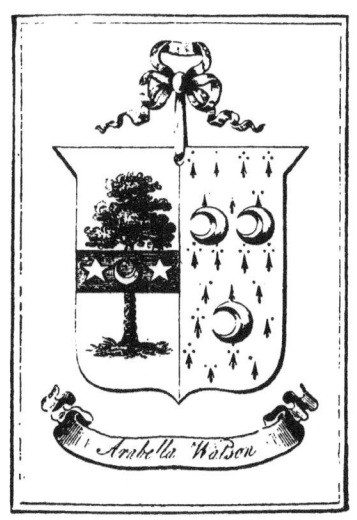

Ladies' Plates

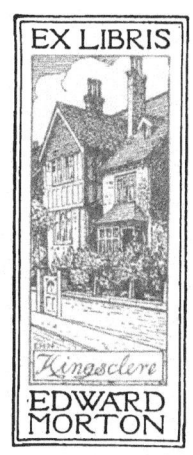

BY E. H. NEW

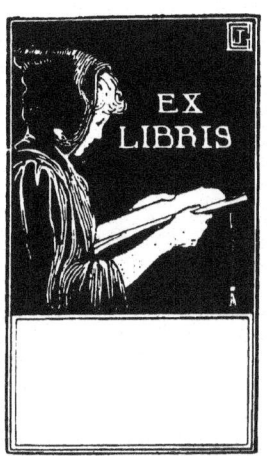

BY J J GUTHRIE

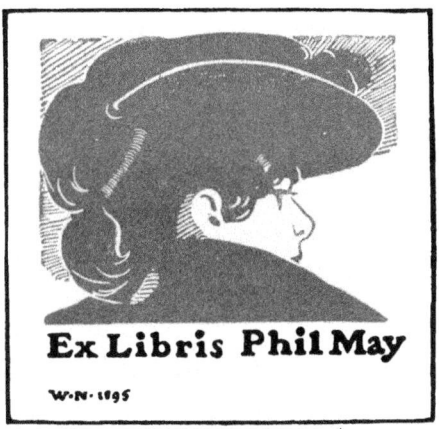

Designed by W. P. Nicholson

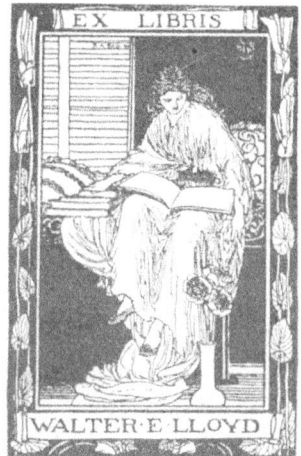

BOOK-PLATE BY R. ANNING BELL

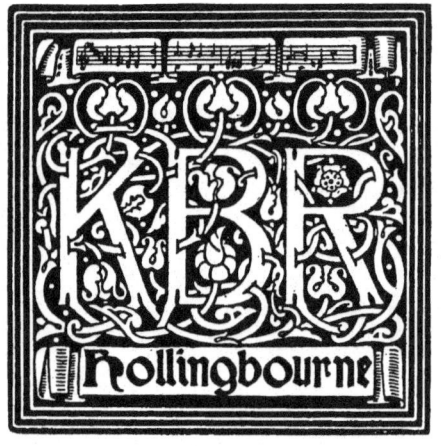

BY E. BENGOUGH RICKETTS

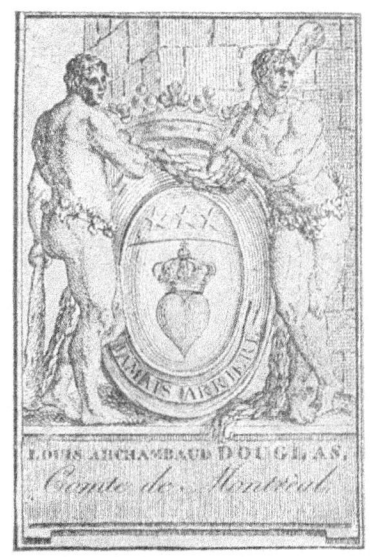

Unknown Designer

(Old)

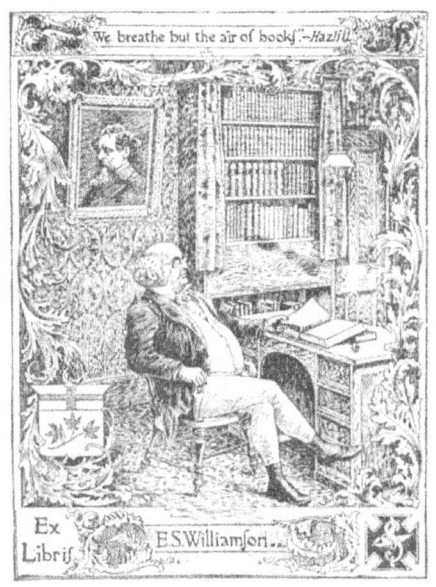

Book-Plate of Mr. E. S. Williamson, Toronto

(Recent)

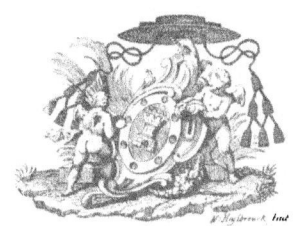

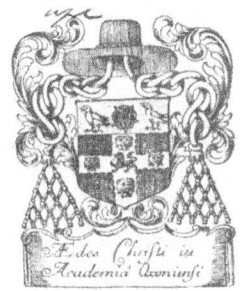

CAROLUS EDUARDUS,

Ecclesiastical Ex-Libris

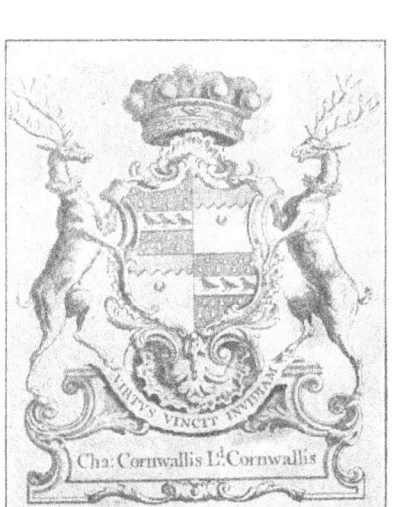

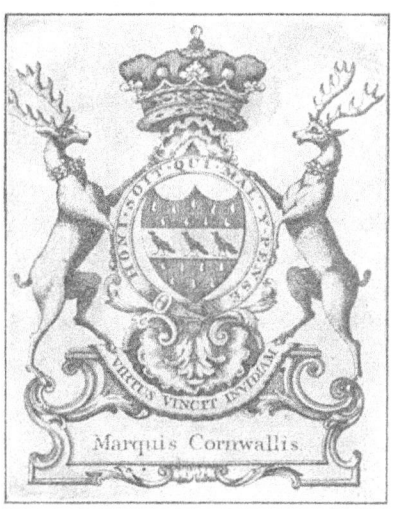

Some collectors include these among their American Plates

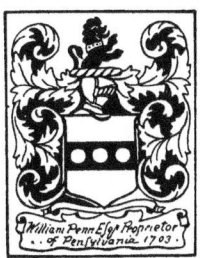

Book-Plate of William Penn, dated 1703

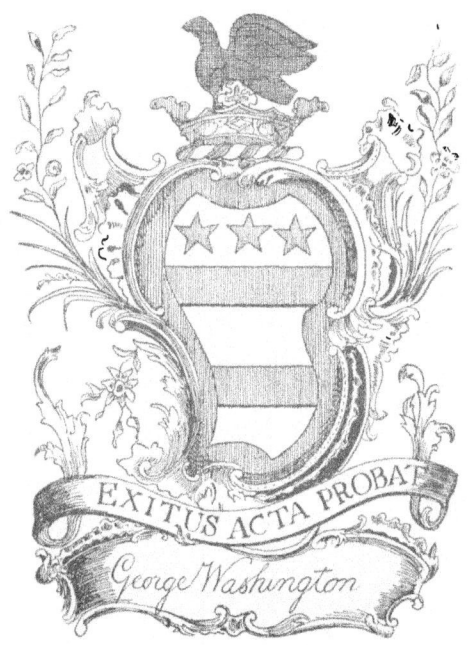

Book-Plate of Washington

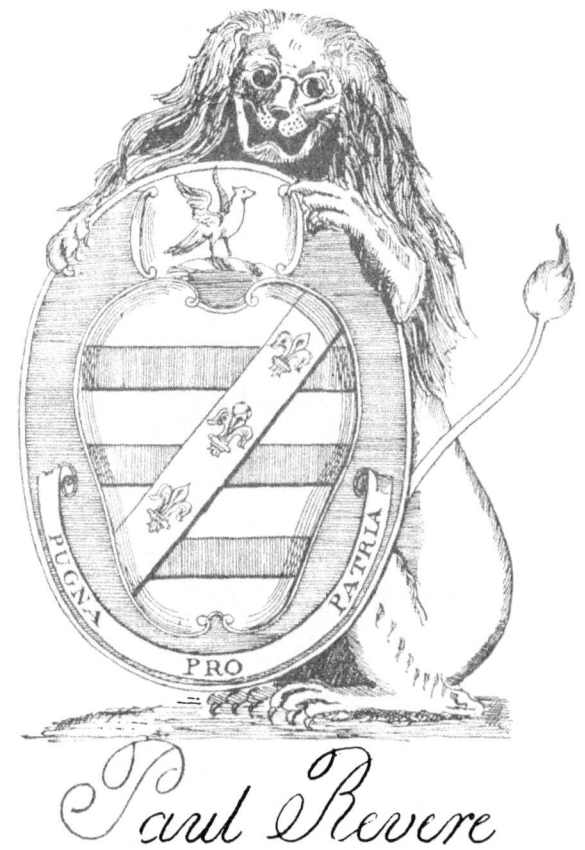

Designed and Engraved by the Owner

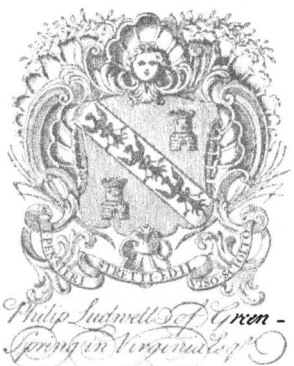

Early American

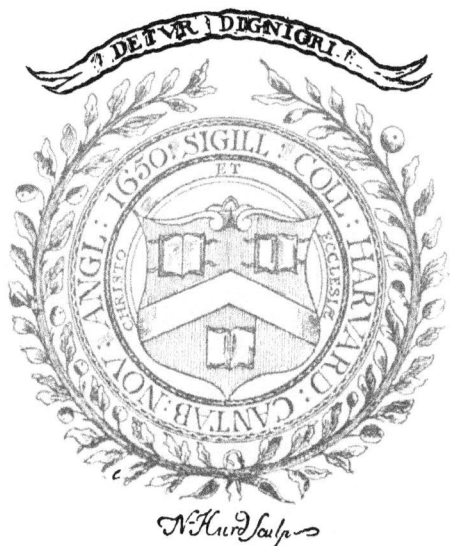

Early College Plates

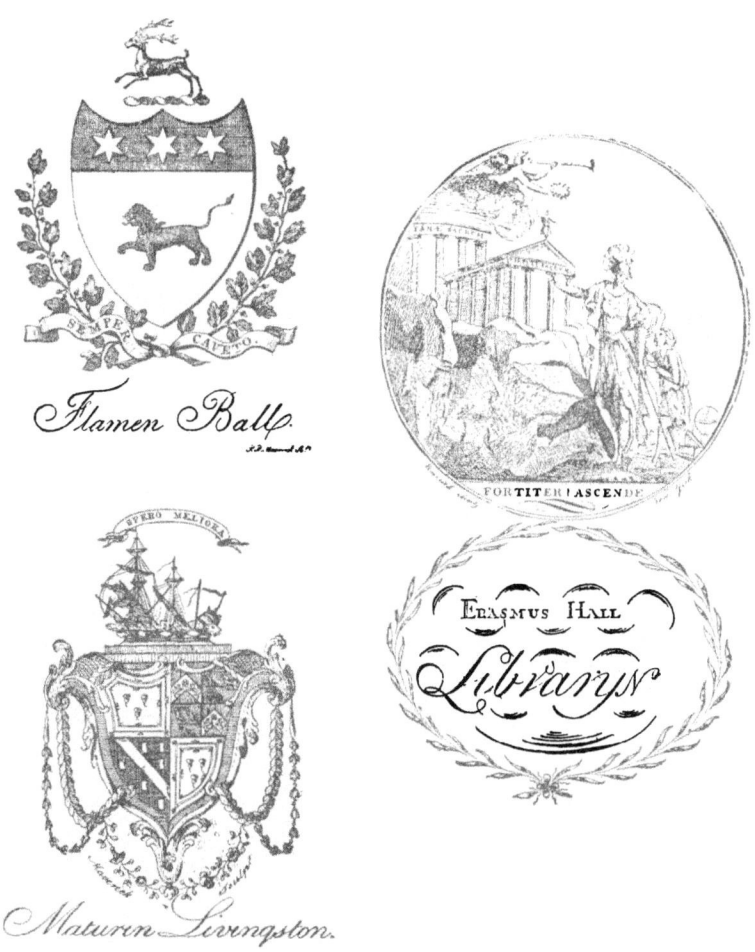

Designed by Peter Rushton Maverick

WASHINGTON
CIRCULATING
LIBRARY,
No. 3568
Corner of Wall & Wm. streets.

B. LEVY AND CO.'S
CIRCULATING
LIBRARY.
No. 3568

GENERAL
CIRCULATING LIBRARY,
SPURRIERGATE, YORK.

Three labels from one volume. The lowest one is the oldest

THE
PROPERTY
OF
JOHN HARVEY,
NEW-YORK
1806.

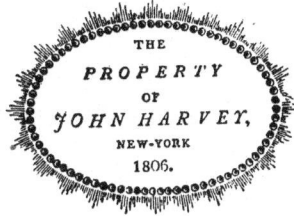

No. 2102   MEHR LICHT   1 Vol

𝔚illiam 𝔄. 𝔖locum.

In these days of book-deluge, keep out of the salt swamps
of literature, and live on a small, rocky island of your own,
with a lake and a stream in it, pure and good.—RUSKIN.

1878   HODIE MIHI CRAS TIBI

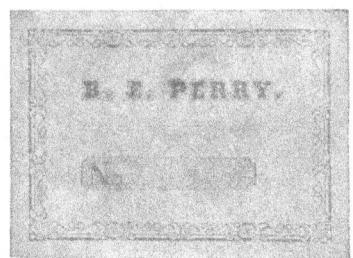

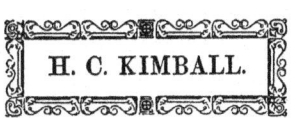
H. C. KIMBALL.

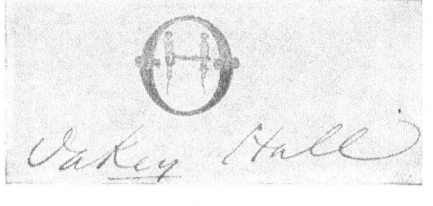

Punning Plate

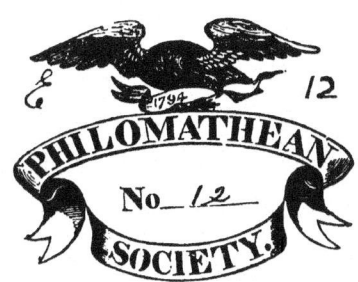

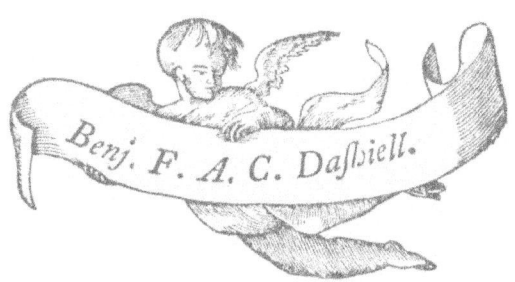

Recently discovered by Walter R. Benjamin, New York

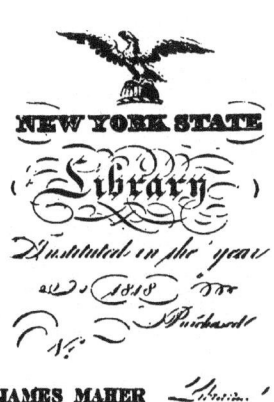

Ornamental Label Book-Plates

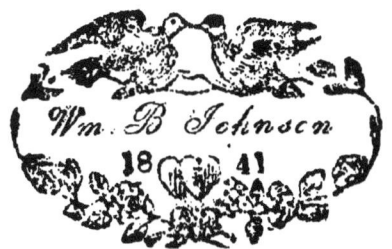

Connecticut Name Label

Noted New York Antiquarian

Ornamental Label Book-Plates

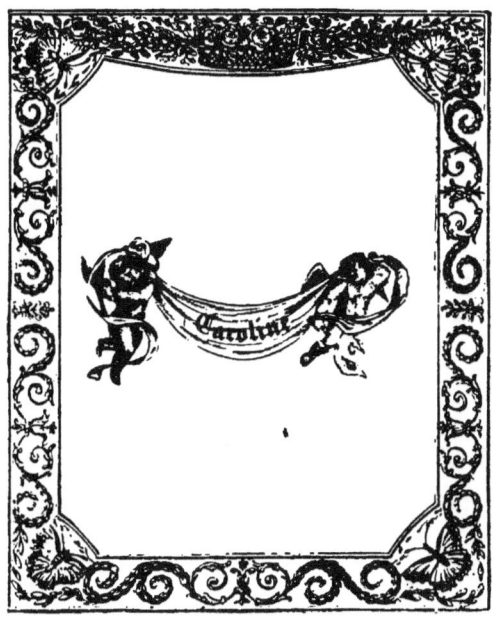

Ladies' Book-Plate

Label Form

[AMERICAN]

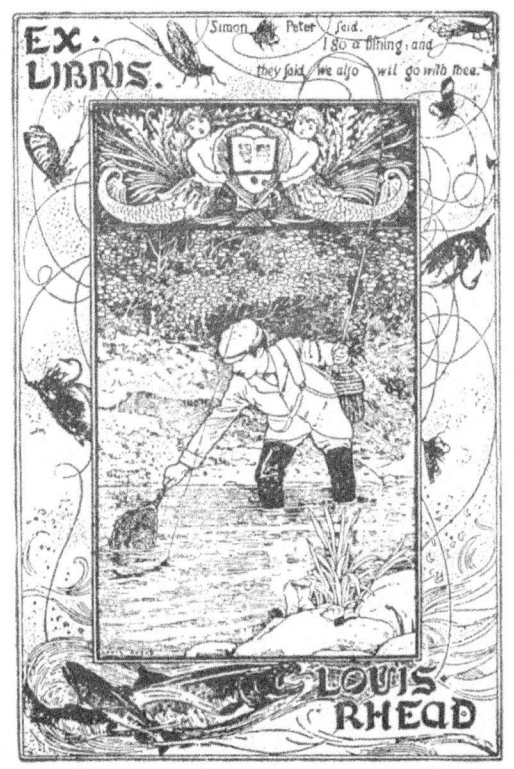

Designed by Louis J. Rhead

135

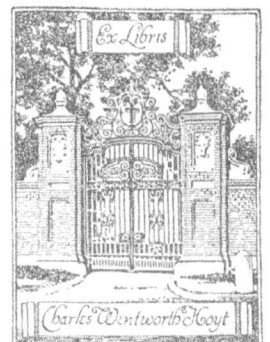

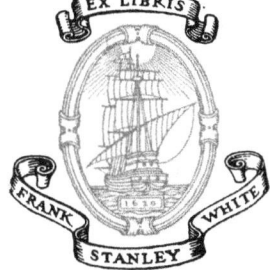

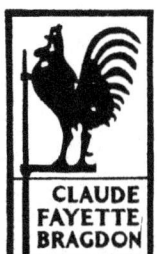

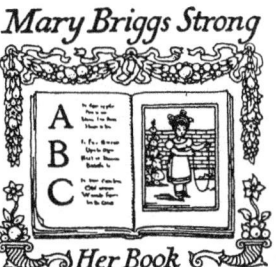

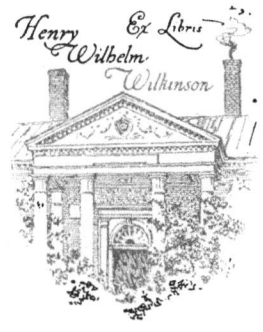

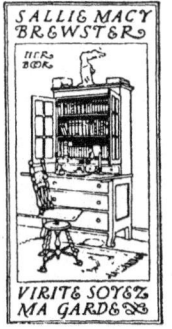

Designed by CLAUDE FAYETTE BRAGDON

[AMERICAN]

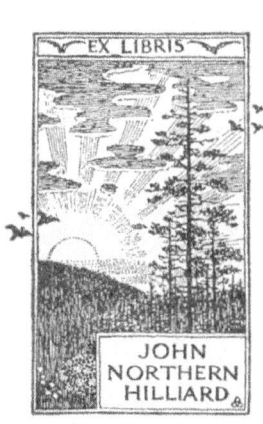

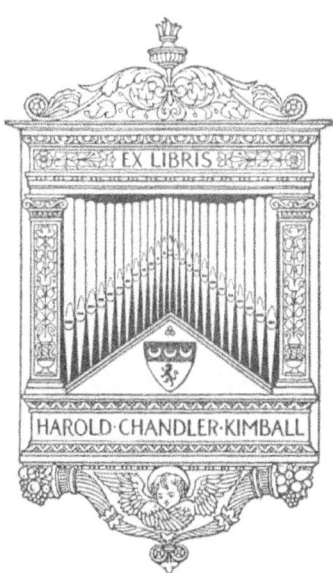

Designed by CLAUDE FAYETTE BRAGDON

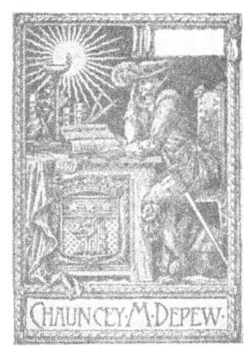
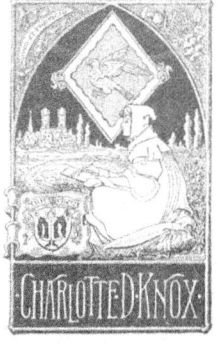
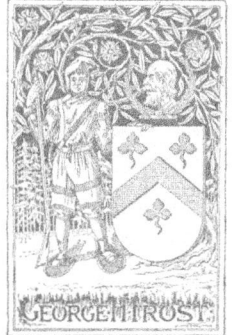

Designed by David McNeely Stauffer

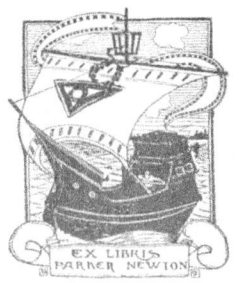

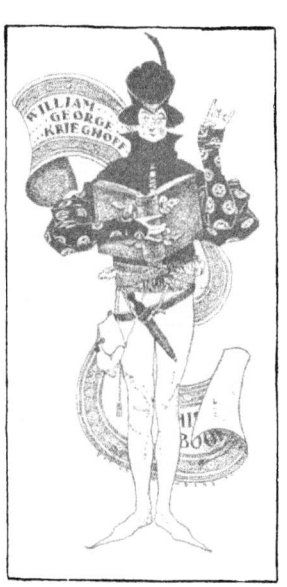

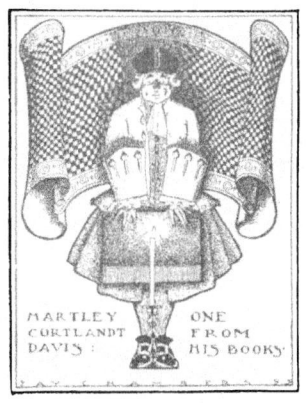

Designed by Jay Chambers

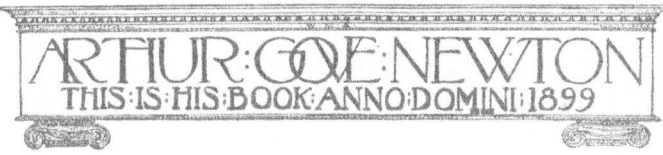

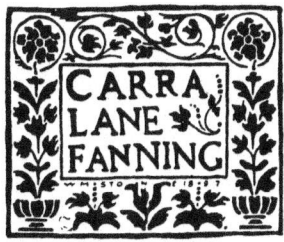

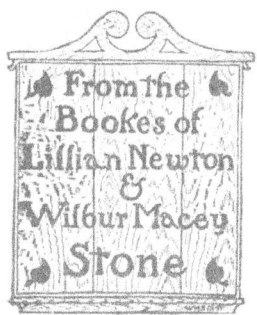

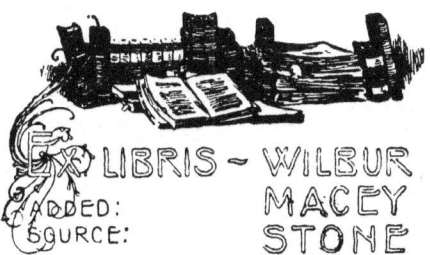

Designed by WILBUR MACEY STONE

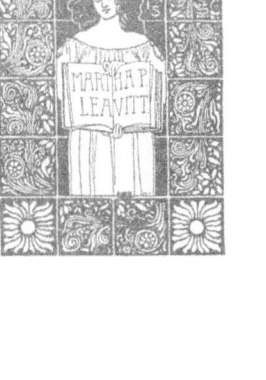

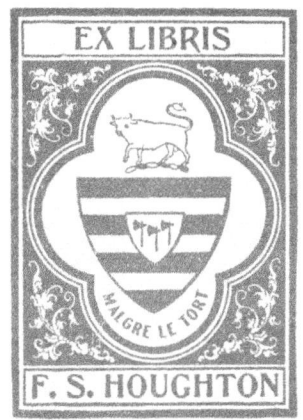

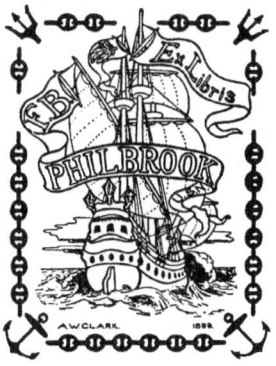

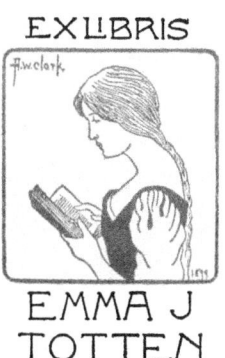

Designed by A. W. Clark

147

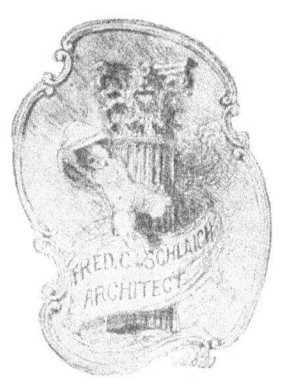

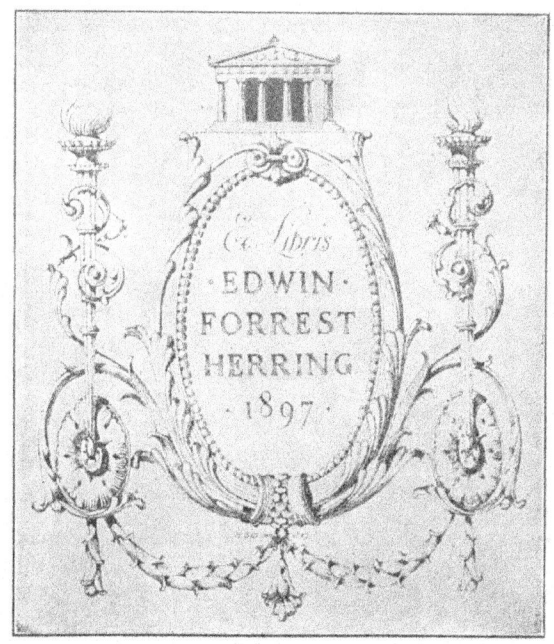

Designed by HOWARD SILL

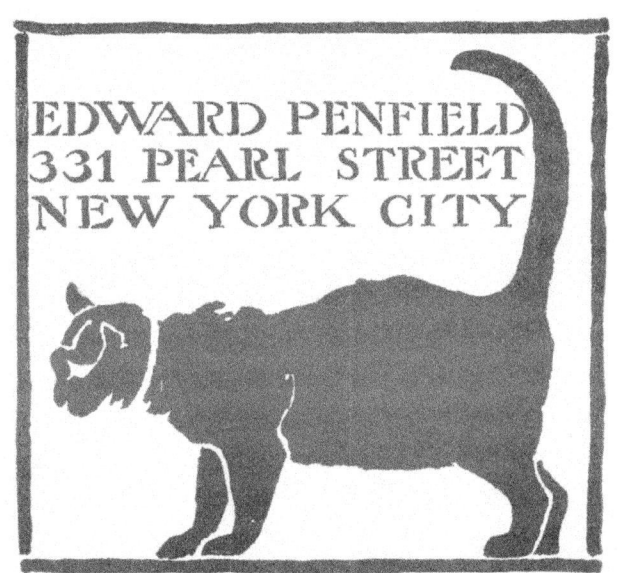

Designed by EDWARD PENFIELD

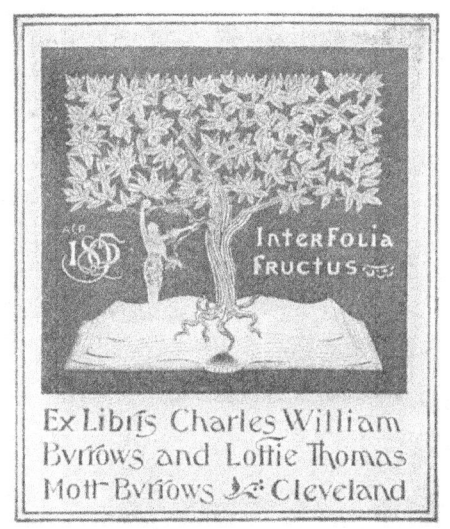

A "Joint" Book-Plate

Designed by A. C. R.

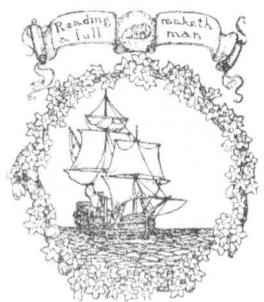

Edwin S.
Crandon

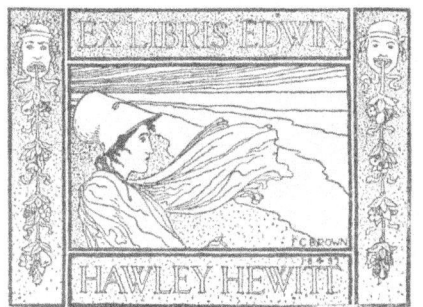

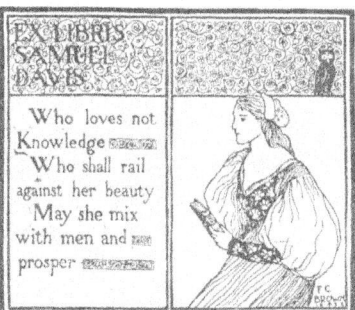

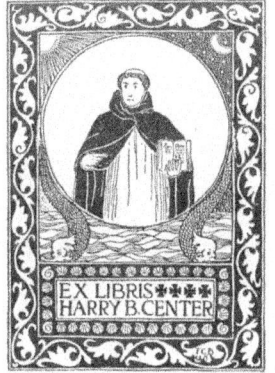

Designed by Frank Chouteau Brown

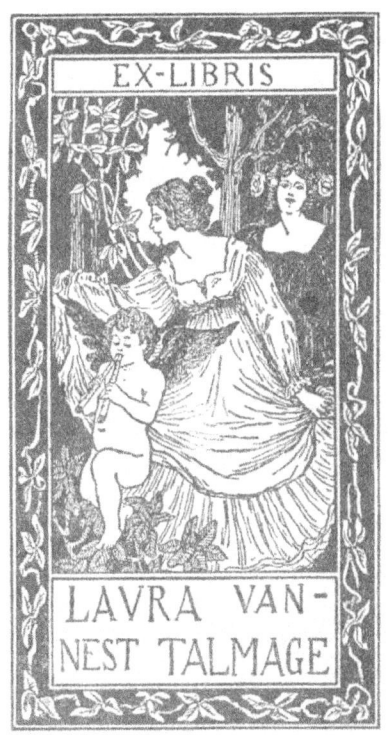

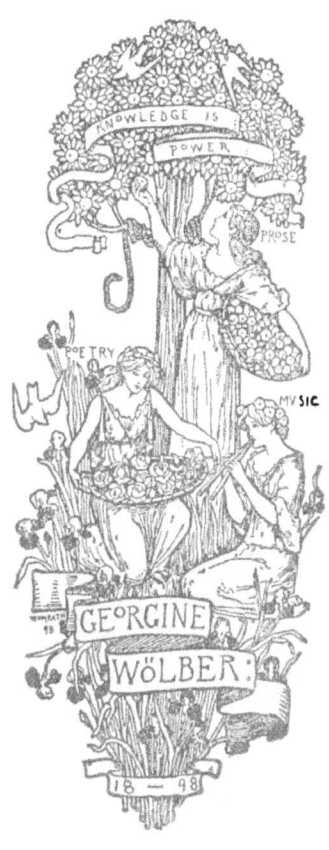

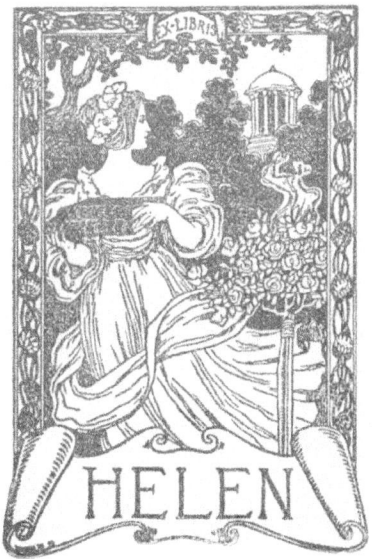

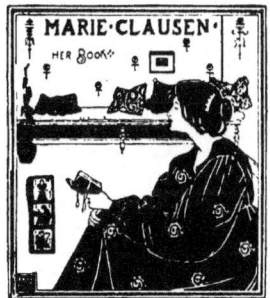

Designed by Andrew Kay Womrath

[AMERICAN]

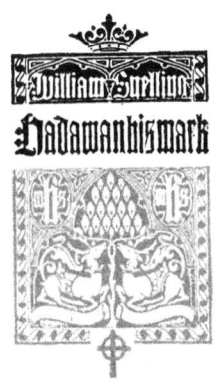
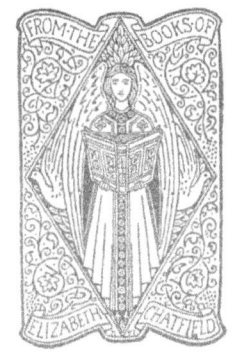
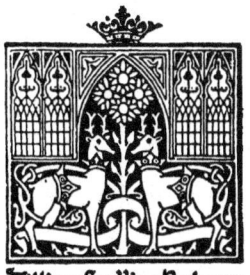

Designed by W. S. Hadaway

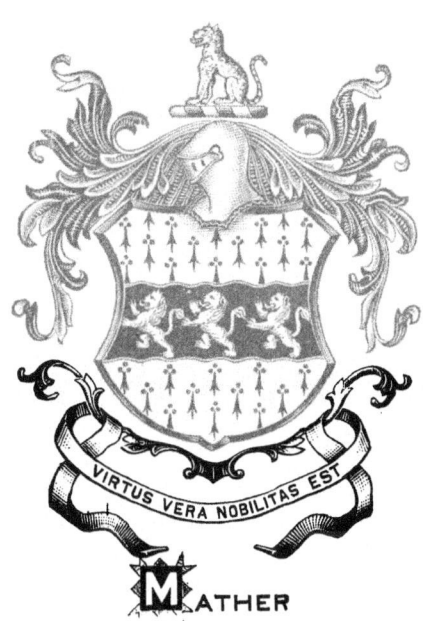

VIRTUS VERA NOBILITAS EST

MATHER

Unknown Designer

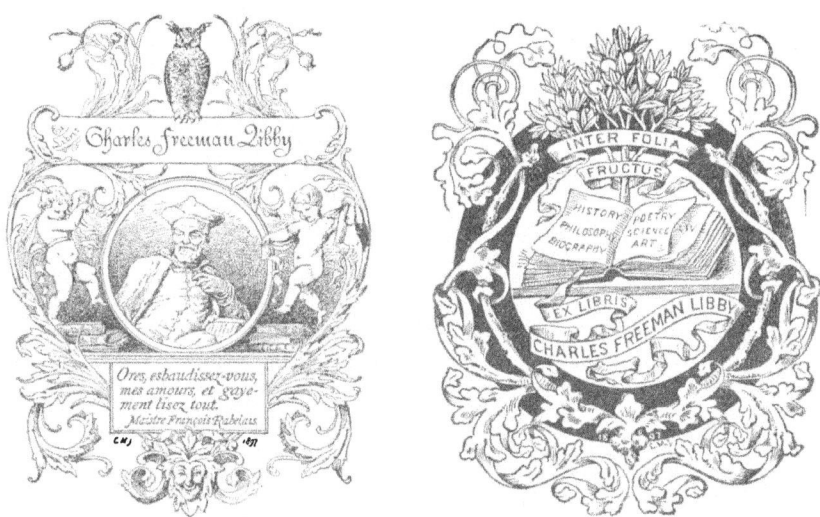

Designed by C. M. JENCKES

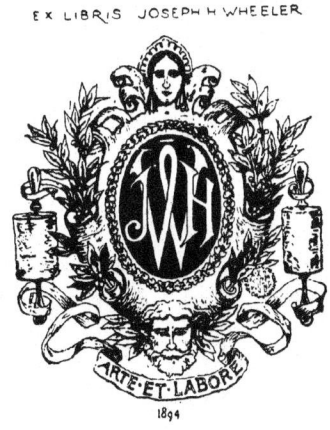

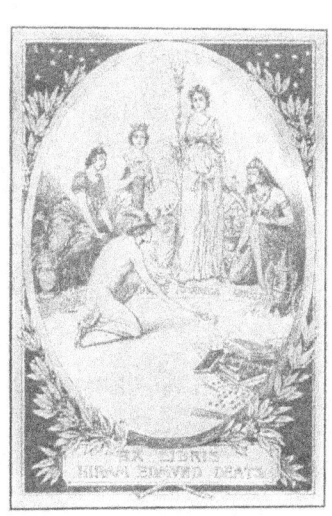

Designed by EDMUND H. GARRETT

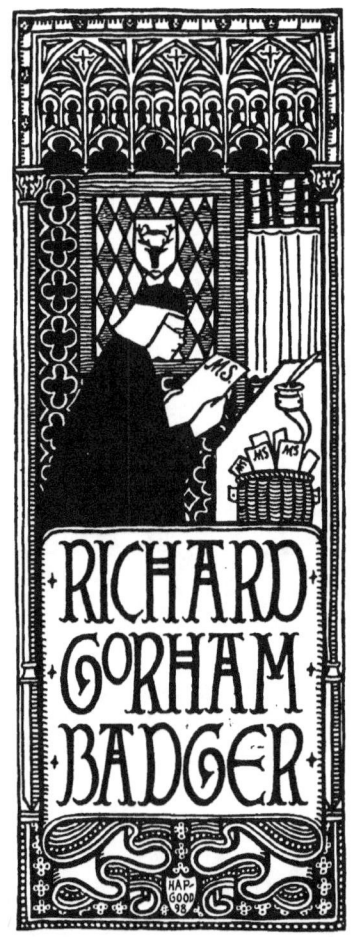

RICHARD GORHAM BADGER

Designed by Theodore Brown Hapgood, Jr

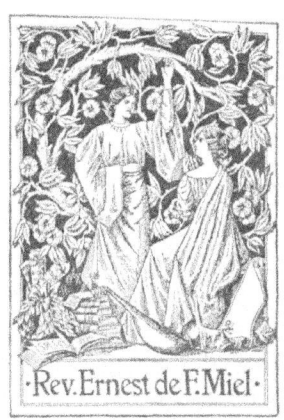

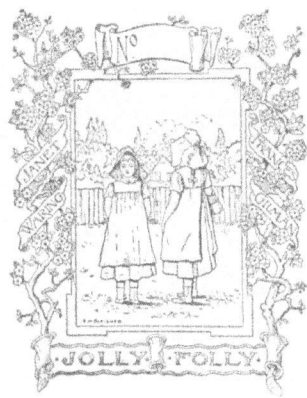

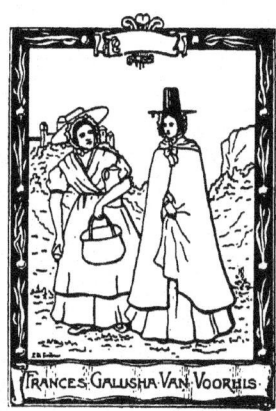

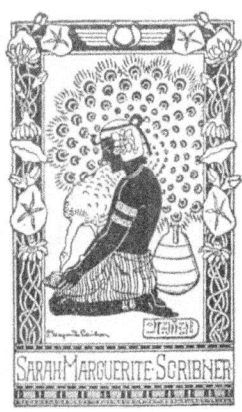

Designed by S. Marguerite Scribner

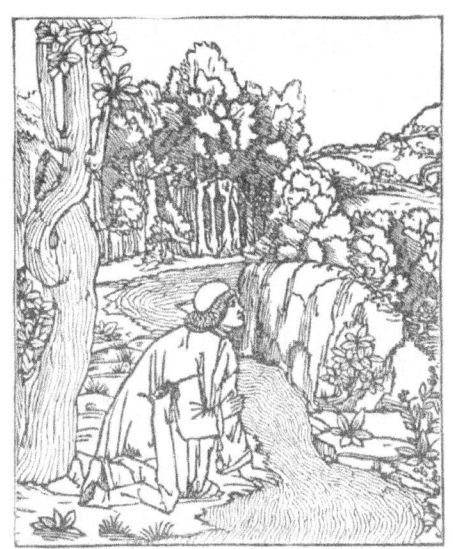

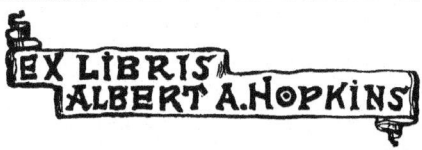

dapted from an early Italian wood-cut

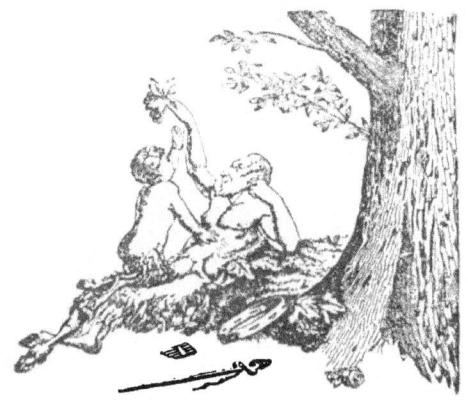

Ex Libris

W G. Bowdoin

Allegoric Book-Plate

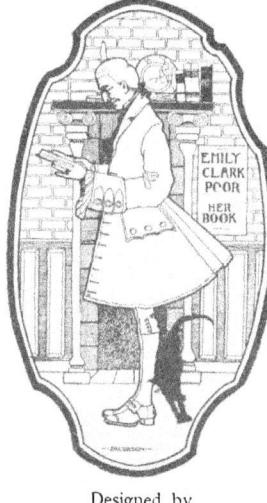

Designed by

F. Arthur Jacobson

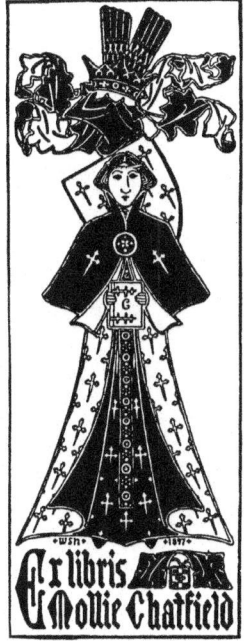

Designed by

W. S. Hadaway

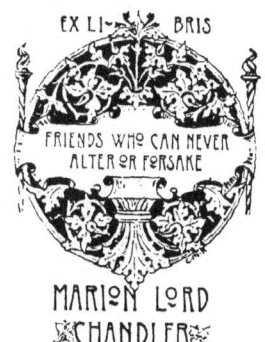

Designed by

Christia M. Reade

[AMERICAN]

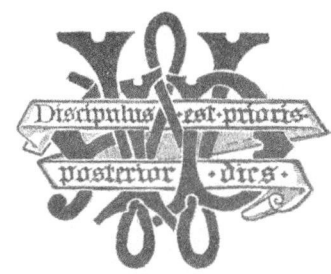

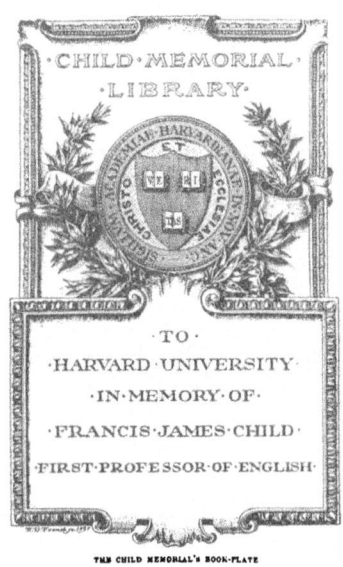

PRESIDENT WHITE LIBRARY,
CORNELL UNIVERSITY.

LENOX LIBRARY

Bancroft Collection.
Purchased in 1893.

THE CHILD MEMORIAL'S BOOK-PLATE

Designed by EDWIN DAVIS FRENCH

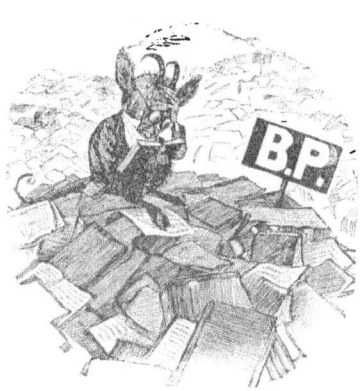

Book-Plate of BARNET PHILLIPS

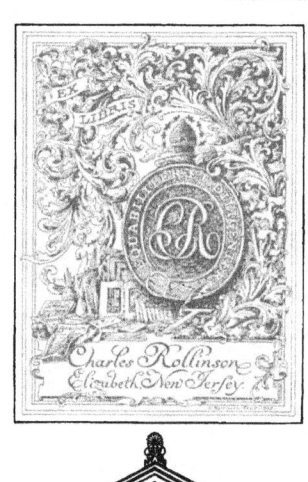

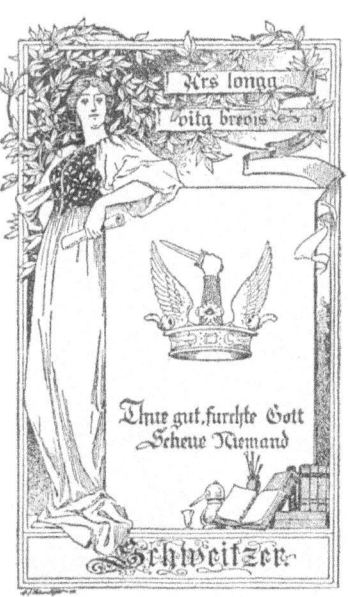

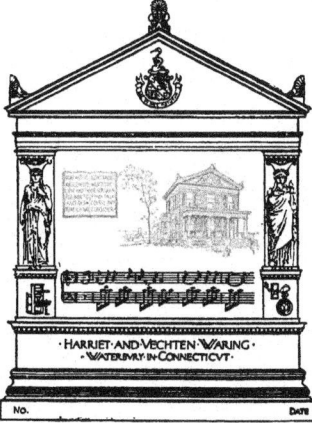

Designed by CHARLES ROLLINSON

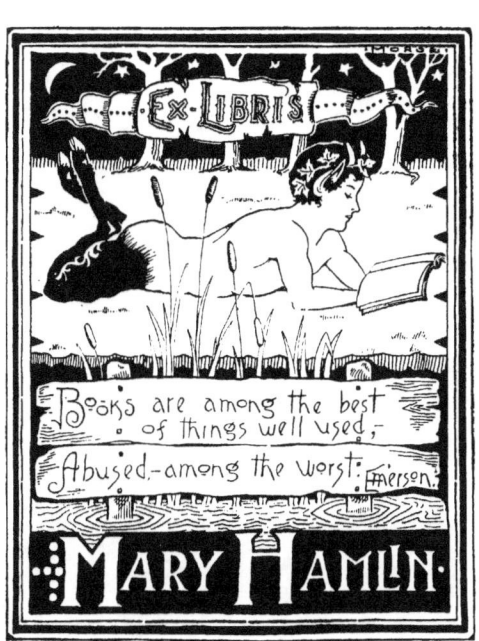

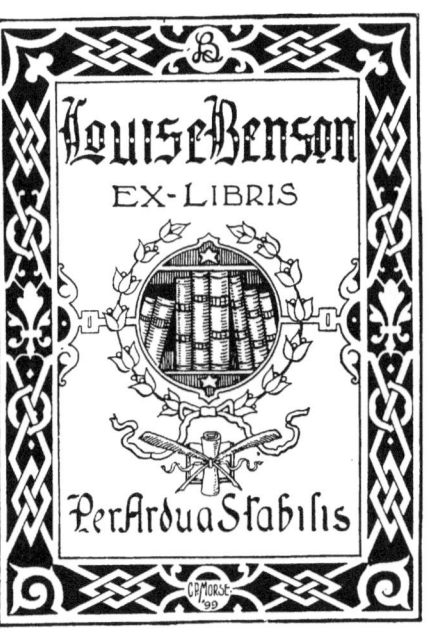

Designed by CHARLES P. MORSE

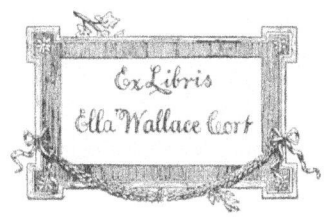

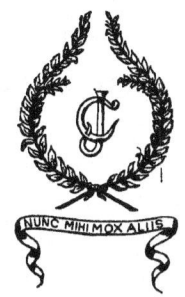

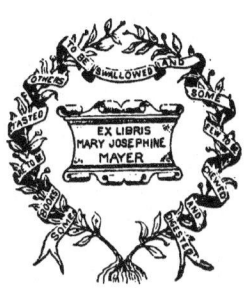

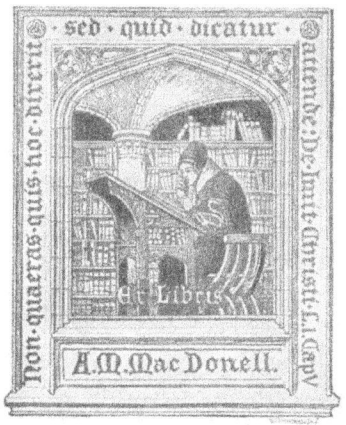

Designed by S. H. Horgan

Collection of Henry Blackwell

177

Designed by F. W. GOUDY

and used in the books contained in the library of " The Alton
Limited " trains between Chicago and St. Louis

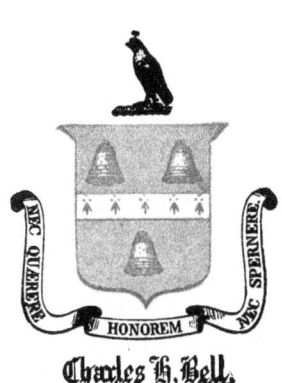

Charles H. Bell.

LIBRARY
of
James A. H. Bell.

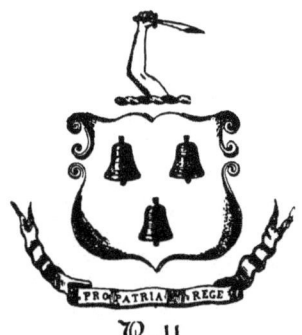

Bell.

179

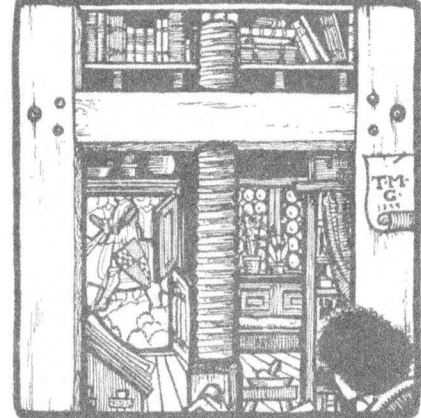

From Among
The Books of

ANGUS
FREDERICK
MACKAY

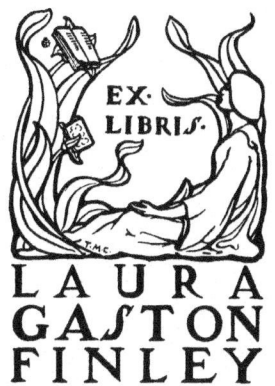

EX·
LIBRIS·

LAURA
GASTON
FINLEY

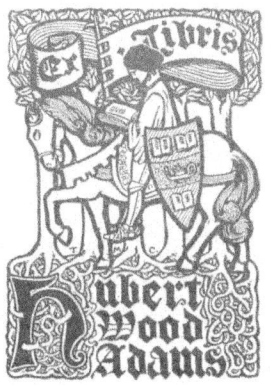

Designed by Thomas Maitland Cleland

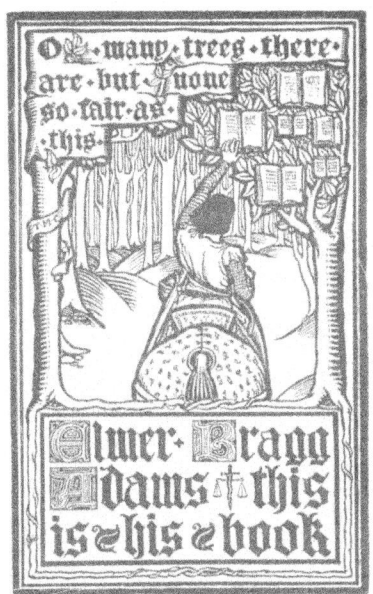

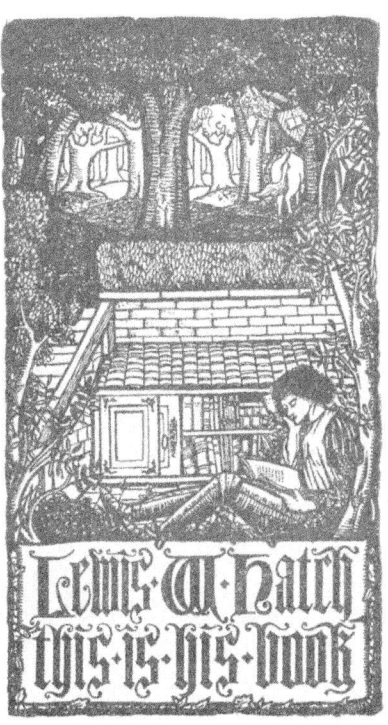

Designed by Thomas Maitland Cleland

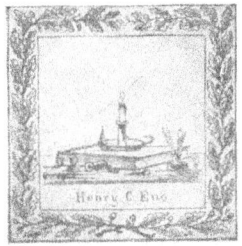

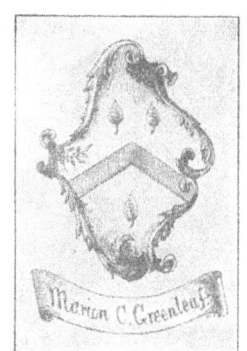

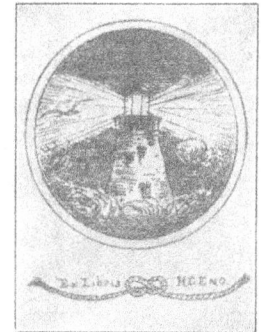

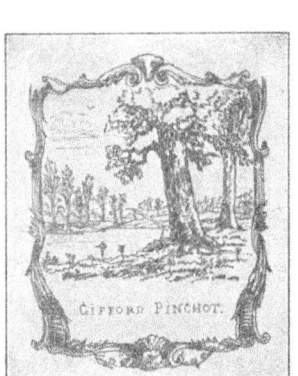

Designed by Dr. HENRY C. ENO

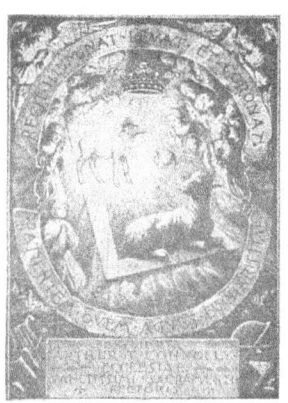

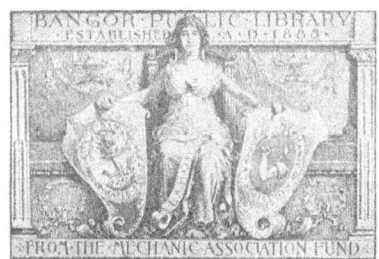
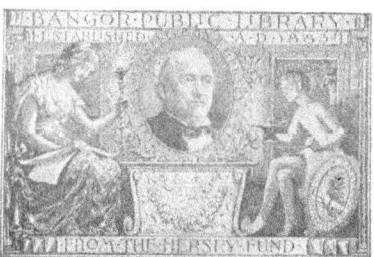

Designed by SIDNEY L. SMITH

187

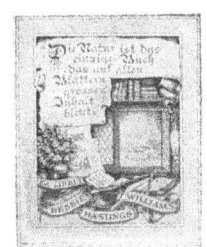

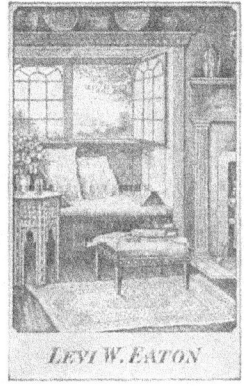

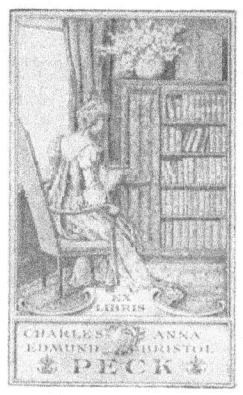

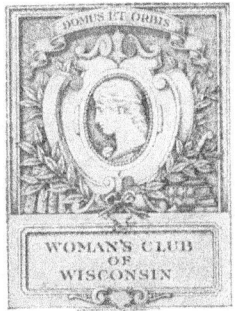

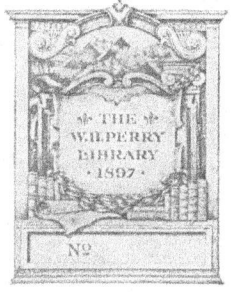

Designed by J. WINFRED SPENCELEY

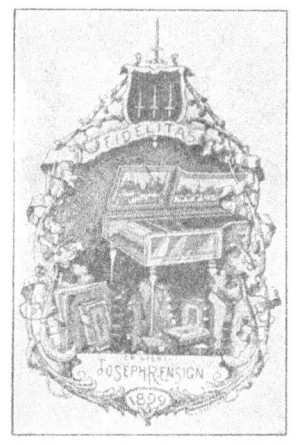

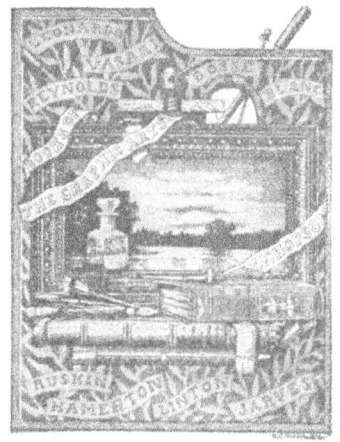

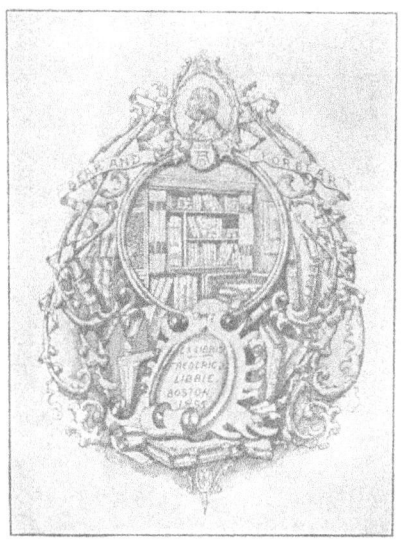

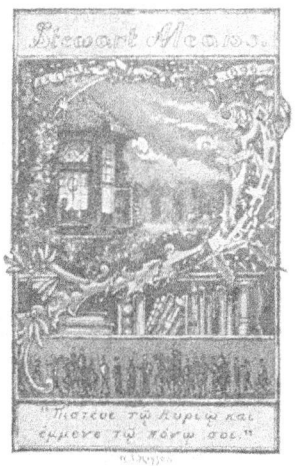

Designed by WILLIAM F. HOPSON

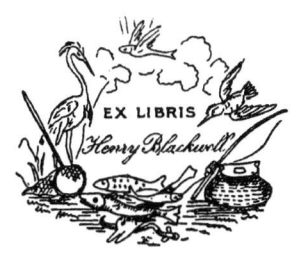

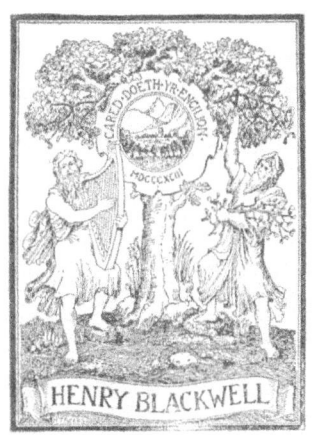

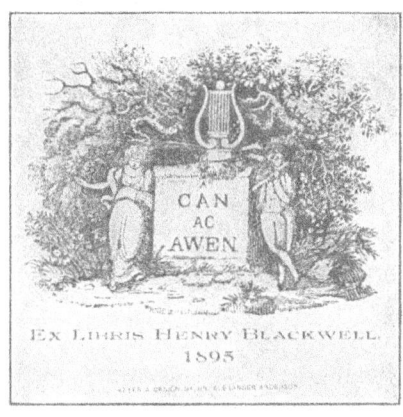

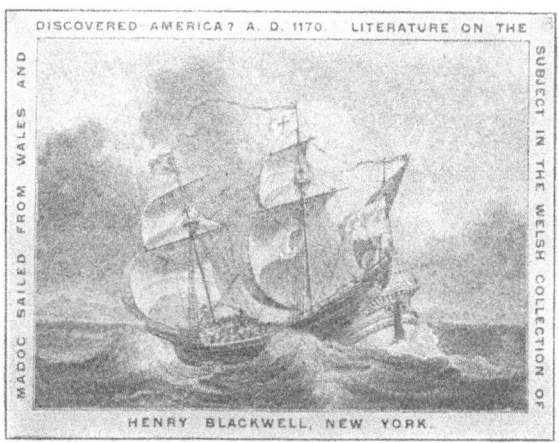

Some of the plates of HENRY BLACKWELL

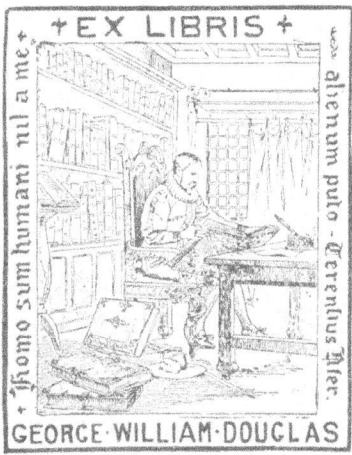

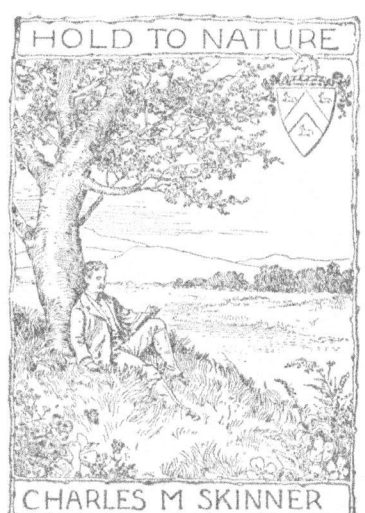

Designed by Orrin W. Simons

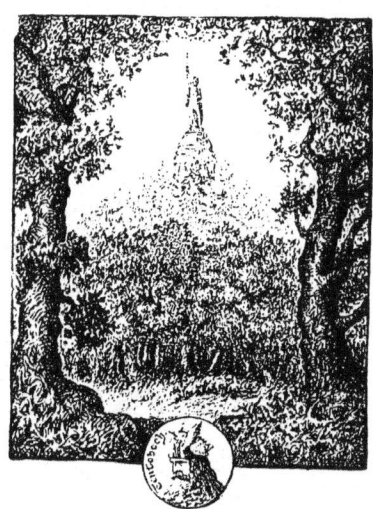

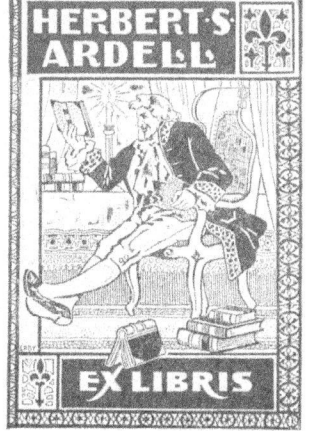

Augustus Toedteberg

Designed by the Owner

Designed by Walter H. Cady

Brooklyn Book-Plates

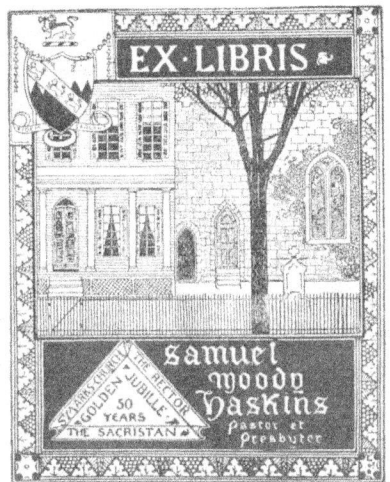

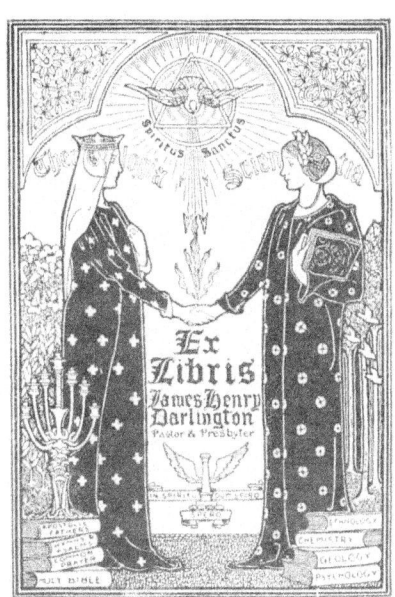

Designed by Louis J. Rhead

Armorial

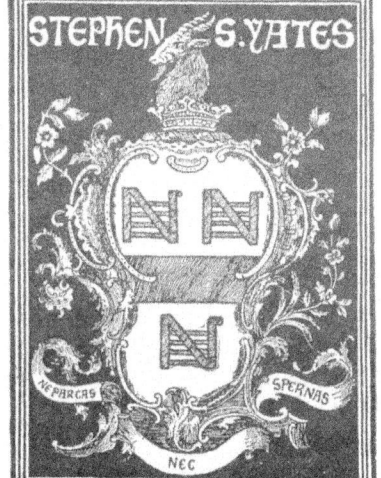

Chippendale

Brooklyn Book-Plates

[AMERICAN]

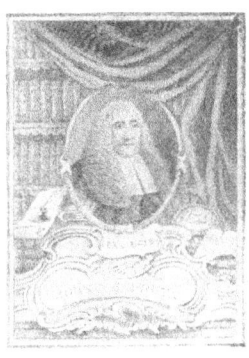

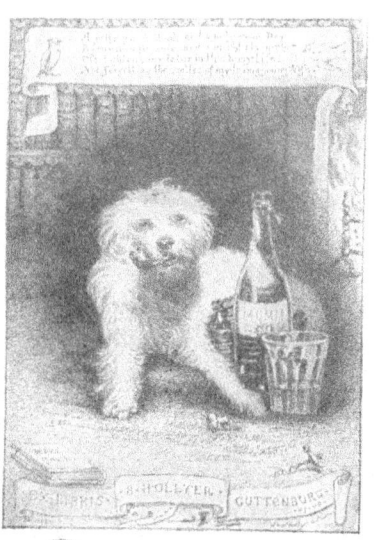

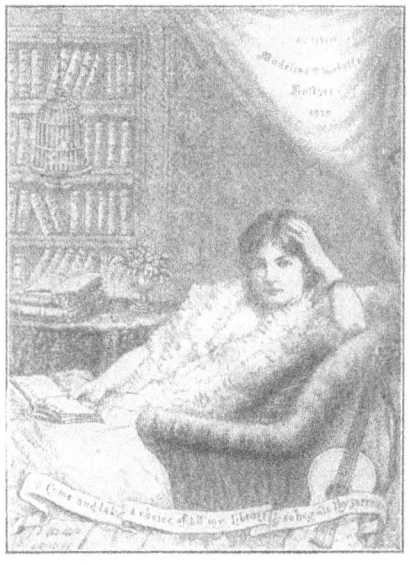

Designed by Samuel Hollyer

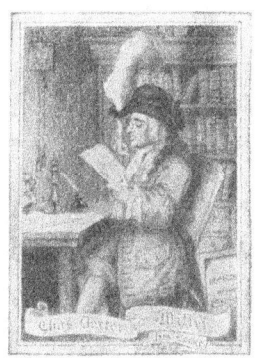

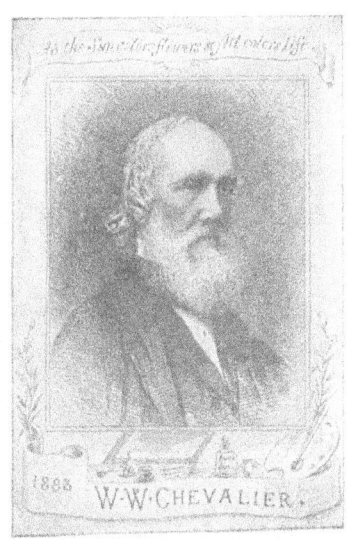

Designed by SAMUEL HOLLYER

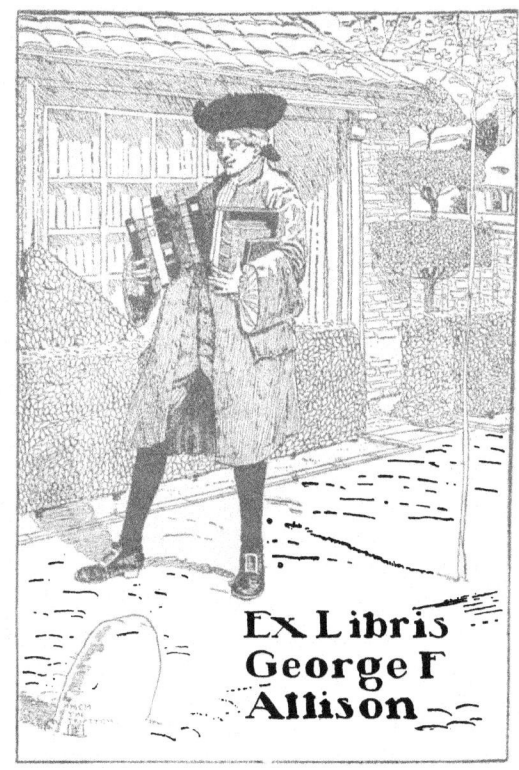

Designed by The Triptych Designers (New York)

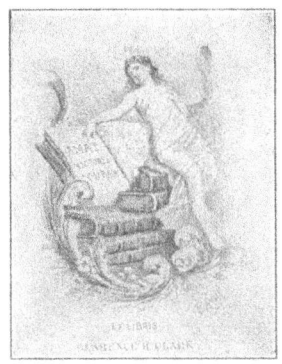

Designed by PAUL AVRIL

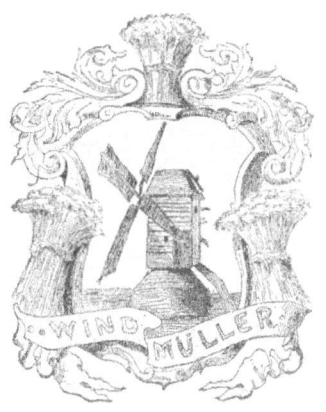

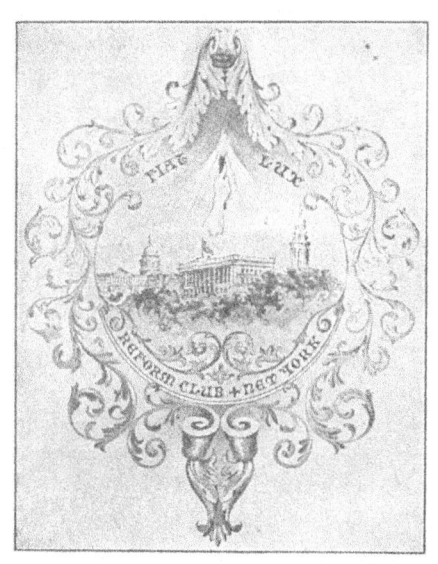

Designed by MISS HURLBURT

[AMERICAN]

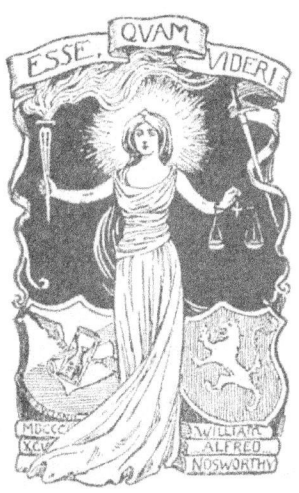

Designed by Florence Pearl England
(Now Mrs. Nosworthy)

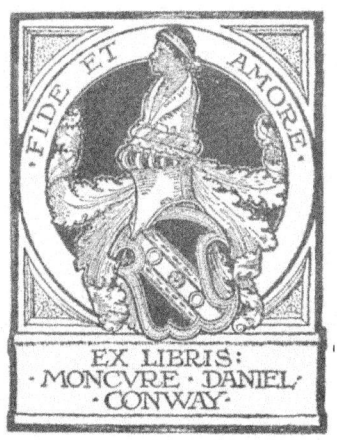